This copy of
# GLOSSARY FOR THE FOOD INDUSTRIES
belongs to:

_____

# GLOSSARY FOR THE FOOD INDUSTRIES

by
**Wilbur A. Gould, Ph. D.**

Consultant to the Food Industries,
Executive Director Mid-America Food
Processors Association,
Emeritus Professor/Former Director
Food Industries Center
The Ohio State University

**CTI Publications, Inc.**
Baltimore, Maryland USA

# GLOSSARY FOR THE FOOD INDUSTRIES

COPYRIGHT© 1990 By **CTI Publications,Inc.**
Baltimore, Maryland USA

CTI Publications, Inc.
2619 Maryland Ave., Baltimore, MD 21218-4576 USA

Printed in the United States of America

Library of Congress Catalog Card Number 90-81543

**ISBN Numbers are as follows:
0-930027-16-7**

While the recommendations in this publication are based on scientific studies and wide industry experience, references to basic principles, operating procedures and methods, or types of instruments and equipment are not to be construed as a guarantee that they are sufficient to prevent damage, spoilage, loss, accidents or injuries, resulting from use of this information. Furthermore, the study and use of this publication by any person or company is not to be considered as assurance that a person or company is proficient in the operations and procedures discussed in this publication. The use of the statements, recommendations, or suggestions contained, herein, is not to be considered as creating any responsibility for damage, spoilage, loss, accident or injury, resulting from such use.

**Additional food industry publications available form
CTI Publications, Inc.:**

*A Complete Course In Canning, 12th Edition
Current Good Manufacturing Pratices/Food Plant Sanitation
Food Production/Management
Total Quality Assurance For The Food Industry*

For information on obtaining copies of these publications
Please contact us at the address below:

# CTI PUBLICATIONS Inc.

2619 Maryland Ave., Baltimore, MD 21218-4576 USA
301-467-3338 ● FAX: 301/467/7434

## PREFACE

This book is an outgrowth of conversations with Joe Pietrowski, AKZO Salt Co., Art Judge, II and Randy Gerstmyer of CTI Publications and Winston D. Bash, The Ohio State University Food Industries Center, and several former students. The latter constantly asked for my definitions so that they could better understand the language of the food industries in some of its broadest sense.

Beyond my own files built up during the last 50 years of active work in the food industries, I have drawn freely from many sources for terms, terminologies, acronyms, and abbreviations that are useful in this industry. The tables in the Appendix are some of the tables that I constantly refer to in dealing with various aspects of the food industries. Further information may be garnered from the listed References. However, I assume full responsibilities for these definitions and I assure you that my search for proper terms and terminologies in this glossary was not done hastily.

As you use this glossary, please send me your suggestions for improving it and for further expansion. Your comments and suggestions will be sincerely appreciated.

Wilbur A. Gould

# GLOSSARY FOR THE FOOD INDUSTRIES

## Contents

# ABBREVIATIONS/ACRONYMS

**a** — Acceptance number of defects in a sampling plan.

**A₂** — A factor in the construction of X Bar chart.

**AAAS** — American Association for the Advancement of Science.

**ACS** — American Chemical Society.

**AEC** — Atomic Energy Commission.

**AFD** — Accelerated Freeze Drying.

**AFDOUS** — Association Food Drug Officials (US).

**AID** — The Agency on International Development (US).

**Alpha** — Probability of rejection, sometimes referred to as the producers risk, or risk of an error of the first kind.

**Amp.** — Ampere.

**AMS** — Agricultural Marketing Service (USDA).

**ANOVA** — Analysis of Variance.

**AOAC** — Association Official Analytical Chemists.

**AOCS** — American Oil Chemist's Society.

**AOM** — Active Oxygen Method, an accelerated rancidity test.

**AOQ** — Average Outgoing Quality.

**AOQL** — Average Outgoing Quality Limit.

**APHA** — The American Public Health Association.

**APHIS** — Animal and Plant Health Inspection Service.

**AQL** — Acceptance Quality Level-associated with vendor's risk.

**ARL** — Average Run Length.

**Ave** — Average (also, indicated by A bar).

**A$_w$** — Water activity- a measure of the available water in a product.

**Beta** — Probability of acceptance, sometimes called the Buyers or Consumers risk, or risk of an error of the 2nd kind.

**BHA** — Butylated hydroxyanisole, an antioxidant.

**BHT** — Butylated hydroxytoluene, an antioxidant.

**BOD** — Biological Oxygene Demand.

**Bu** — Bushel.

**BTU** — British Thermal Unit-The quantity of heat needed to raise 1 lb. of water 1 degree F.

**c** — Number of defects or defective units.

**c Bar** — Average number of defects in a sample.

**C** — Centigrade or Celsius.

**ca** — Circa or about.

**CA** — Controlled Atmosphere.

**CAD** — Computer Aided Design.

**CAM** — Computer Aided Manufacturing.

**cc** — Cubic Centimeter, a measure of volume (0.0338 ounce).

**CIE** — Official name of the International Committee on Illumination.

**CIP** — Cleaned in Place.

**cm** — Centimeter (1/1000 of a Meter or 0.394 of an inch).

**CGMP** — Current Good Manufacturing Practice.

**COD** — Chemical Oxygen Demand.

**COP** — Cleaned Out of Place.

**CSIRO** — Commonwealth Scientific and Industrial Research Organization.

**CUSUM** — Cumulative Sum Sampling Plan for attributes standards only.

**CV** — Coefficient of Variability.

**cwt** — Hundred weight.

**$d_2$** — A divider of the mean range, R Bar, which will yield an estimate of the standard deviation.

**$D_3$** — A multiplier of R Bar to determine the 3 sigma lower control limit on a range chart.

**$D_4$** — A multiplier of R Bar to determine the 3 sigma upper control limit on a range chart.

**DAL's** — Defect Action Levels.

**d. f.** — Degrees of freedom.

**D value** — Time to destroy 90% of spores or vegetative cells of a microorganism at a given temperature. Number of minutes for the survivor curve to traverse one log cycle.

**DSIR** — Department of Scientific and Industrial Relations (US, Canada, and the British Commonwealth).

**EDTA** — Ethylendiamine tetraacetate salts, a powerful sequestrant added to fat type foods.

**F** — Fahrenheit.

**F** — Frequency.

**F value** — Defined as number of minutes required to destory a stated number of microorganisms at a defined temperature, usually at 250 degree F.

**FAO** — Food and Agriculture Organization (US).

**FIFO** — First In First Out.

**$F_0$** — The number of equivalent minutes at a temperature of 250 degree F. to inactivate a microbial population with a z value at 18 degree F. for *Clostridium botulinum*, $F_0 = 12D$.

**FAO** — The Food and Agricultural Organization.

**FDA** —Food and Drug Administration (US).

**ffa** — Free Fatty Acid.

**g** — Gram (0.035 oz.) (453.6 g = one lb.).

**GATT** — General Agreement on Tariffs and Trade.

**GMP** — Good Manufacturing Practice.

**gpm** — Gallon per minute.

**GRAS** — Generally Recognized As Safe.

**HDL** — High Density Lipoprotein.

**HFI** — Hold for Investigation.

**HACCP** — Hazard Analysis Critical Control Points.

**HTST** — High Temperature Short Time.

**hp** — Horsepower.

**IU** — International unit of measure.

**IFT** — Institute of Food Technologists.

**IQF** — Individually Quick Frozen.

**IPM** — Integrated Pest Management.

**IU** — International Unit.

**JIT** — Just In Time.

**kg** — Kilogram (1000 grams) or (2.2046 lb).

**kw** — Kilowatt (1000 watts).

**L** — Lower Specification Limit.

**LDL** — Low Density Lipoprotein.

**LBO** — Leveraged Buy Out.

**LCL** — Lower control limit on a control chart.

**LIFO** — Last In First Out.

**LSD** — Least significant difference.

**M** — Meter (1000 Millimeters on 39.700 inches).

**M** — Molar.

**MDR** — Minimum Daily Requirement.

**Me** — Mean.

**mg** — Milligram (1/1000 of a gram).

**Ml** — Milliliter (cubic centimeter) (0.03382 oz).

**mm** — Millimeter (1/1000 of a meter).

**MO** — Mode.

**MSNF** — Milk Solids Not Fat.

**mv** — Millivolt (1/1000 of a volt).

**MVTR** — Moisture Vapor Transmission Rate.

**n** — The number of items or observations in a given lot, that is, the Sample.

**N** — Number of items in a given lot to be sampled.

**N** — Normal solution.

**NAS** — National Academy of Science.

**NIH** — National Institute of Health.

**NRC** — National Research Council.

**OCC** — Operating Characteristic Curve.

**OSHA** — Occupational Safety and Health Administration (US).

**Oz** — Ounce (1/16 of a lb) (28.35 grams = one oz.).

**p** — Average proportion defective for the process.

**PCB's** — polychlorinated bi-phenyls, a class of compounds known to cause cancer.

**PER** — Protein Efficiency Ratio.

**pH** — Hydrogen ion concentration.

**POC** — Price of Conformance.

**PONC** — Price of Non-Conformance.

**ppm** — parts per million (1 ppm = 0.0001% by wt.)

**psi** — pounds per square inch.

**PUFA's** — Polyunsaturated Fatty Acids.

**Pt** — Pint.

**PV** — Peroxide value, a measure of oxidative rancidity of oils or products.

**QA** — Quality Assurance or Quality Audit.

**QC** — Quality Control.

**QC** — Quality Circle.

**QE** — Quality Evaluation.

**Qt** — Quart.

**QWL** — Quality of Work Life.

**r** — Symbol for the correlation coefficient.

**$r_2$** — The square of the correlation coefficient, also known as the coefficient of determination.

**R** — Range, the difference between the largest value and the smallest value in a set of numbers.

**R Bar** — The average of the ranges.

**RDA** — Recommended Daily Allowance (US).

**RH** — Relative Humidity.

**ROI** — Return on Investment.

**rpm** — Revolutions per minute.

**RQL** — Reject Quality Level.

**s** — Standard Deviation.

**$S_2$** — Mean variance.

**SFI** — Solids Fat Index.

**SPC** — Statistical Process Control.

**SPC** — Standard Plate Count.

**Sp.Gr.** — Specific Gravity.

**SQC** — Statistical Quality Control.

**TBA** — Thiobarbituri acid, a measure of oxidative rancidity.

**TBHQ** — Tertiary butylated hydroquione, an antioxidant.

**tbsp** — Tablespoon.

**TDT** — Thermal Death Time.

**TQA** — Total Quality Assurance.

**TQI** — Total Quality Improvement.

**TQM** — Total Quality Management.

**tsp** — teaspoon.

**TVP** — Texturized Vegetable Proteins.

**U** — Upper Specification Limit.

**UCL** — Upper control limit on a control chart.

**UHT** — Ultra High Temperature.

**USDA** — United States Department of Agriculture.

**USDC** — United States Department of Commerce.

**USDI** — United States Department of Interior.

**USP** — United States Pharmacopeia.

**Vol** — Volume.

**X** — A number representing the value of a single item.

**X Bar** — Average.

**X Double Bar** — Average of the averages.

**WHO** — World Health Organization (UN).

**Wt.** — Weight.

**z Value** — Temperature range (degree F.) necessary for the D value to change by a factor of 10 or for one log cycle reduction in a specific microbial population.

**A la** – Phrase meaning prepared according to a given style.

**A la carte** – Menu term for items individually priced and may be made to order rather than a complete meal.

**A la king** – Dish of cooked chicken, sweet peppers and mushrooms in a veloute sauce.

**A la mode** – Prepared according to a particular fashion, such as pie topped with ice cream.

**Absorption** – Retention or holding or incorporation of oil or fat by a food product which has been fried.

**Acceptance** – An experience, or feature of experience characterized by a positive attitude. May be measured by preference or liking for specific food item.

**Acceptance Number (C)** – The maximum number of deviants permitted in a sample of a lot that meets a specification.

**Accompaniments** – Salads, bread, vegetables, pickles, jams or relishes— Items that accompany the main meal.

**Acidophilus Milk** – Comparable to Bulgarian Milk-prepared by fermenting sterile skim milk inoculated with *Lactobacillus acidophilus.*

**Acetic Acid** – The acid of vinegar. Formed by the bacterial fermentation *(Acetobacteria aceti)* of alcohol.

**Acid** – A substance in which the hydrogen ion concentration is greater than the hydroxyl ion. May be organic or inorganic. Generally sharp and sour taste.

**Acidified Foods** – Low-acid food to which an acid or an acid food is added to produce a food with a final equilibrium pH of 4.6 or less and a water activity greater than 0.85.

**Acidity** – The pH of a liquid or solid between 7.0 and 1.0.

**Acidulant** – An acid added to a food to aid in preservation or modify taste.

**Aciduric** – Organisms that can be grown in high acid foods.

**Acrid** – A substance that is sharp and harsh or bitterly pungent.

**Acuity** – Ability to discern or perceive stimuli, sharpness or acuteness.

**Additive** – Any substance, the intended use of which results or may reasonably be expected to result directly or indirectly in its becoming a component or otherwise affecting the characteristics of any food (FDA).

**Adjuvants** – Materials used with sprays to achieve penetration, sticking, spreading or wetting.

**Adsorption** – To take up or hold on the surface, e.g., oil on potato chips.

**Adsorbent** – Material on whose surface adsorption takes place.

**Adulterate** – To make a substance or product impure by mixing in a foreign or inferior substance or product.

**Aerobes** – Organisms which require oxygen or air for growth.

**Aflatoxin** – A series of organic substances which have been invaded by the fungal species *Aspergillus Flavus* or *A. Parasiticus* and deposited in corn kernels.

**Agar** – A gelatinous colloid used for culture medium or a stabilizing agent.

**Agglomeration** – The forming of a mass by causing a product to be dispersed throughout another product.

**Agitating Cookers** – Retorts or cookers which provide product agitation during processing.

**Albumen –** The white of an egg, composed primarily of the protein albumin.

**Albumin –** Simple proteins that are soluble in water and coagulated by heat, e.g., egg whites, blood and milk.

**Aldehyde –** A class of organic compounds characterized by the presence of the unsaturated carbonyl group ($C=O$).

**Algae –** A group of lower plants having chlorophyll but no vascular system, examples are seaweed, that is, kelp the major source of carrageenan.

**Alginate –** Salt of alginic acid found in seaweed-used as thickeners and stabilizers.

**Alkali –** A substance that has basic properties, that is, a pH in excess of 7.0

**Alkaloid –** Bitter nitrogen containing compounds usually found in seed plants.

**Allergy –** A hypersensitivity to a specific substance or condition which in similar amounts is harmless to most people.

**Allspice–** Dried fruits of the pimento.

**Ambrosia –** Sweet tasting liquor or rich desert.

**Ameliorate –** To balance must by adding sugar, water, and/or grape concentrate.

**Amioca –** Starch obtained from waxy-maize grain (corn).

**Amino acids –** Any of numerous nitrogen containing acids, 22 of which are building block of proteins. 8 of these 22 amino acids are essential amino acids, that is they must be obtained outside of the body as part of the diet.

**Amlopectin –** A branched polysaccharide found in starch.

**Ampere –** The rate of current flow, that is, Ampere= volt/ohm.

**Amylase –** An enzyme that hydrolizes starch and glycogen to maltose.

**Amylose** – A straight chain polysaccharide found in starch.

**Amylography** – An instrument employed to measure the response of starch suspensions to heating under controlled conditions with the obtained data having a direct relationship to the performance of soft wheat flours for given applications.

**Anerobes** – organisms which grow in the absence of oxygen or air.

**Antibiotic** – A substance that inhibits the growth of microorganisms usually produced by other organisms such as penicillin.

**Anticaking agent** – Substance used in many salts and powders to keep them free-flowing.

**Antifoamer** – Liquid of low intrinsic surface tension that prevents formation of a foam.

**Antimicrobial** – A compound which inhibits the growth of a microbe.

**Antioxidant** – A substance that retards or slows down oxidation of organic substances.

**Antipasto** – Term meaning before the meal and used to describe appetizers.

**Antimycotic** – A substance which destroys or inhibits the growth of molds and other fungi.

**Appertif** – A short drink of an alcoholic beverage including wines with added essenses and flavors of spices, herbs, roots, etc. offered before dinner to increse the appetitie. Vermouths are an example.

**Appetite** – The desire of or craving for food.

**Appetizer** – A food used to introduce a meal or stimulate the appetite and it may include canapes, cocktails or hors d'oeuvres.

**Aquaculture** - Culture of foods in water.

**Aroma** - Generally pleasing odor or fragrance.

**Asepsis** - The absence of viable organisms.

**Aseptic** - Free of disease or spoilage causing organisms.

**Aseptic Processing** - The filling of a commercially sterilized-cooled product into pre-sterilized containers, followed by aseptic hermetic sealing with a pre-sterilized closure in an atmosphere free of microorganisms.

**Ash** - The residue of a substance which has been incinerated at about 525 degree C (975 degree F).

**Aspic** - Term used to indicate the arrangement of food into a molded gel.

**Astringent** - Perceived quality caused by shrinkage, drawing, or puckering of the skin surfaces of the mouth, that is, dry feeling of the mouth usually due to tannins. (phenolic compounds).

**Atmosphere** - A measure of pressure.

**Atom** - The smallest particle of an element that exhibits the properties of that element.

**Atomic Number** - The number of protons in a nucleus of an element ranging from 1 for hydrogen to 106. The number indicates the position of an element in the periodic table and determines its chemical properties and behavior.

**Atomic Weight** - The mass (weight) of an atom of an element-Carbon equals 12.

**Attribute** - An inherent characteristic of a product classified as acceptable or unacceptable.

**Attributes** - A method of measurement whereby units of products are examined for the presence or absence of specified characteristics in each unit in the sample.

**Au fait** - Brick of ice cream with layers of frozen fruit.

**Au Gratin** - Covered with cheese and cooked.

**Au jus** – Juice obtained from roasting and served with the product.

**Available Chlorine** – The amount of active chlorine in a chlorine bearing compound that can be released in a water solution. Chlorine as a gas is totally available chlorine.

**Average** – The sum of a number of measurements divided by the number of units.

**Avoirdupois** – A system of weights based on the pound of 16 ounces and the ounce of 16 drams.

# B

**Bacilli –** Rod shaped bacteria.

**Bacteria –** Single celled microscopic organisms which usually produce by splitting in two (called fission). There may be several shapes, that is, rods, spherical(cocci), filamentous, etc. Many types are infectious, but others are beneficial.

**Bactericidal –** Destructive to bacteria.

**Bacteriostatic –** Preventing the growth of bacteria without killing them.

**Bake –** To cook by dry heat in an oven.

**Baking Soda –** Leavening agent which acts through release of carbon dioxide during baking.

**Banquet –** A meal taken in company of others.

**Barbeque –** To cook in a highly seasoned vinegar sauce usually over coals or in a spit.

**Base –** Alkaline substance, that is, one with a pH greater than 7.0.

**Baste –** To moisten with liquid while cooking.

**Batter –** A soft liquid basically of flour and a liquid.

**Baume –** A hydrometer scale used to measure the density of a liquid.

**Beaded Can –** A can which is strengthened by reinforcing ribs or concentric depressions around the body of the can.

**Bearnaise –** A thick meat or fish hot sauce made of eggs, butter, vinegar, tarragon and seasonings.

**Beat –** To stir thoroughly and vigorously.

**Beer –** Yeast fermented malt beverage.

**Beurre –** Butter.

**Biodegradable** – Capable of being broken down into innocuous products by microorganisms.

**Bisque** – A thick creamy soup.

**Bitter** – A basic taste response, usually harsh and acrid.

**Blackened** – A food item (meat, fish, poultry, etc.) that has been coated with sugar, cajun spices, and salt and grilled black in a "white hot" pan.

**Blanc** – A mixture of water and flour in which various substances, such as, white meat and certain light colored vegetables are added.

**Blanching** – A unit operatiin in food processing in which raw food materials are immersed in hot water or exposed to live steam, hot gases or microwave energy.

**Blaze** – To flame spirits or wine in cooking.

**Bleaching** – A treatment given to remove natural pigments and other impurities in refining oils.

**Blend** – To mix thoroughly.

**Boeuf** – Beef.

**Boil** – To heat a liquid or to cook in water or other liquid until it reaches 212 degree F or 100 degree C at sea level.

**Boiling Point** – The temperature at which a liquid vaporizes.

**Bombe** – A ball shaped dessert or confection.

**Botulism** – Acute food poisoning caused by the toxin of *Clostridium botulinum*.

**Bordelaise** – A sauce made of red wine, shallots, thyme and pepper.

**Bouillabaisse –** Highly seasoned fish stew made of at least two kinds of fish.

**Bouillon –** A French term for stock or broth, a clear soup usually made from beef.

**Bound water –** Water that is chemically tied to the food.

**Bouquet –** The fragrance or aroma that characterizes a fine wine or other alcoholic beverages.

**Bouquet garni –** A combination of herbs tied together in thin cloth, used to season foods such as soups and stews; usually removed before serving.

**Brainstorming –** A form of creative thinking. It is designed to get unrestricted ideas about a particular topic from all members of a group.

**Braise –** To brown in small amount of hot fat and then cooked slowly in a covered vessel, adding a small amount of liquid.

**Bran –** The outside protective shell of any grain.

**Bread –** To coat with flour or crumbs and egg or liquid prior to cooking.

**Breakdown –** General term describing the onset or progress of undesirable chemical or physical changes in a fat or oil. This may include darkening, formation of excess free fatty acids or peroxides, polymerization and gumming and undesirble foaming. Further, undesirable flavors and odors may develop.

**Break Point Chlorination –** The point (time) in the addition of chlorine to water beyond which where chloramines are oxidized and where future increases in the chlorine dosage will result in a proportional increase of a chlorine residue.

**Brew –** A method of preparation involving steeping, boiling, and fermenting to extract the flavor.

**Brine –** Water with salt, usually sodium chloride. Maximum saturation is 26%.

**Brix –** A measure of the density of a solution, that is, Degree Brix = percent sucrose at 20 degree C.

**Brix Hydrometer –** A hydrometer used for testing the strength of density of a sugar solution.

**Broasting –** A pressure oil cooking process, that is, frying under pressure.

**Brochette –** Skewer or spit made of metal or wood on which chunks of food are fastened before broiling.

**Broil –** To cook directly under heat or over an open fire.

**Broth –** An extract from cooking meat, vegetables, grain etc.

**Brown –** To cook in a small amount of fat until brown.

**Browning –** Discoloration of the cut surfaces of some fruits and vegetables due to enzymatic action.

**Brunch –** Late breakfast, early lunch or a combination of both.

**Buckle –** Defect of a can which results in a permanent distortion of the end.

**Budding –** A method of reproduction of yeast.

**Buffer –** A mixture of compounds which, when added to a solution, protects it from any substantial change in pH.

**Buffet –** A meal in which the dishes are placed on a tiered sideboard, often set at entrance to dining area, on which various dishes of meats, poultry, fish, cold cuts, sweets, pastries, etc. are served in a decorative manner with the diners serving themselves and eating either standing up or seated informally.

**Buffer Capacity –** The ability of a food to resist change in its pH level.

**Bulb crops –** Chives, Garlic, Leek, onions, and shallots.

**Bulgar –** Cracked wheat that has been partially cooked and then toasted.

# C

**"C" Enamel** – An interior coating applied to metal cans to prevent discoloration of foods containing Sulfur compounds.

**Cabaret** – An establishment where drinks, food, and entertainment are offered.

**Cacciatora** – Means "hunter style", popular American version of chicken stewed with tomatoes and/or onions, garlic, anchovies, wine and vinegar.

**Cafe** – Establishment where, in principle, only liquid refreshments are served.

**Caffeine** – A plant alkaloid which acts as a stimulant, found in coffee, cola, and tea. It increases pulse rate, accelerates heart action and may cause high blood pressure.

**Cajun** – A hot, spicy form of cooking for foods using red peppers.

**Calcium** – One of the body minerals needed for bone growth and structure. Calcium assists in blood clotting.

**Cake** – A baked mixture of flour, milk, egg, sugar, flavoring and leavening agent.

**Calorie** – A unit of measuring the value of foods for producing heat and energy in the human body equivalent to the amount of heat required to raise the temperature of one kilogram of water one degree Centigrade.

**Can, Sanitary** – Full open-top can. The can may be drawn or manufactured all in one piece or it may have a double seamed bottom, thus a two piece container. The lid, cover, or top end is double seamed after filling.

**Can, Sanitary** — Continued

*The following terms and definitions are used with the metal container and the sealing of same:*

Body – The principal part of a container, usually the largest part in one piece comprising the sides. It may be round, cylindrical, or other shapes.

Body Hook – The flange of the can body that is turned down in the formation of the double seam.

Bottom Seam – The double seam of the can end put on by the can manufacturer. Also, known as the "factory end".

Chuck – Part of a closing machine which fits inside the end counter-sink and acts as an anvil to support the cover and body against the pressure of the seaming rolls.

Closing Machine (Double Seamer) – Machine used to double seam the can end onto can bodies.

Countersink Depth – The measurement from the top edge of the double seam to the end panel adjacent to the chuck wall.

Compound – A sealing material consisting of a water or solvent emulison or solution of rubber, either latex or synthetic rubber, placed in the curl of the can end. During the seaming operation, the compound fills spaces in the double seam, sealing them against leakage thus effecting a hermetic seal.

Cover – The end applied to the can by the packer. Also, known as the top, lid, packer's end, and canner's end.

Cover Hook – That part of the double seam formed from the curl of the can end.

Cross Over – The portion of a double seam at the juncture with the lap or side seam of the body.

Curl – The extreme edge of the end or cap which is turned inward after the end is formed.

Cut Code – A fracture in the metal of a can end due to improper embossing.

Cut-Over – A break in the metal at the top of the inside portion of the double seam.

**Can, Sanitary** — Continued

Dead Head – An incomplete seam resulting from the chuck spinning in the end countersink during the double seaming operation. Also known as a spinner, skidder, or slip.

Double Seam – The closure formed by interlocking and compressing the curl of the end and the flange of the can body.

Droop – A smooth projection of the double seam below the bottom of the normal seam.

False seam – A double seam where a portion of the cover hook and body hook are not interlocked.

First Operation – The operation in which the curl of the end is tucked under the flange of the can body to form the cover hook and body hook, respectively.

Flange – The outward flared edge of the can body that becomes the body hook in the double seaming operation.

Gasket – Pliable material between cover and container sealing surface designed to maintain a hermetic seal.

Knockdown Flange – A common term for a false seam where a portion of the body flange is bent back against the body without being engaged with the cover hook.

Lap – The section at the end of the side seam consisting of two layers of metal bonded together rather than being double seamed at that point.

Paneling – Condition when the sides of the can are drawn in permanently.

Pinholding – Tiny holes in the metal food container usually caused by external rusting or internal attack of the product on the container.

Seam Thickness – The maximum dimension of the double seam measured across or perpendicular to the layers of the seam.

Seam Width (Length or Height) – The maximum dimension of the double seam measured parallel to the folds of the seam.

**Can, Sanitary —** Continued

Second Operation – The finishing operation in double seaming. The hooks formed in the first operation are rolled tightly against each other in the second operation.
Side Seam – The seam joining the two edges of the body blank to form a can body.
Wrinkle (Cover Hook) – A waviness occurring in the cover hook from which the degree of double seam tightness is determined.

**Canapes –** Small pieces of fried or toasted bread with seasoned toppings.

**Can Code –** A means of identifying individual containers of food. The code is embossed in the can or spray painted on the container.

**Canola Oil –** Oil from the rapeseed plant.

**Carbonation –** The process of dissolving carbon dioxide gas in water utilizing temperature and pressure.

**Carbonated beverages –** Soft drinks, major ingredients are sugar, flavorings, colors, acids, water, and carbon dioxide.

**Capability Index –** ($CP_K$) An index that measures the impovement of the process as firms seek greater uniformity around the desired target. It is calculated by dividing the specification width by the process width. The greater the number the better the index.

**Caramelize –** To melt granulated sugar in skillet over medium heat, stirring constantly, until it becomes a golden brown syrup.

**Carbohydrate –** A chemical compound composed of carbon, hydrogen, and oxygen (Starch, sugar and cellulose are the most common).

**Carbohydrate –** Nutrients that supply energy.

**Carcinogen** – A substance that causes cancer in animals or man.

**Carotenoids** – A class of natural occurring pigments.

**Carrageenan** – A coloidal carbohydrate found in seaweeds.

**Case** – The number of containers ordinarily packed in a shipping container.

**Casein** – Milk protein.

**Casserole** – A dish prepared as a mixture of meats, fish, vegetables, seasonings, etc. and baked in a glass or ceramic container, usually with a cover.

**Catalase** – An enzyme. A substance that undergoes no chemical change itself, but which accelerates or affects chemical reaactions.

**Catalyst** – A substance that speeds up a reaction without undergoing any permanent chemical change.

**Catechol** – An enzyme found in plant tissues.

**Cause, assignable** – A factor contributing to variation that can be identified. In statistical process control, assignable causes must be found and removed.

**Cause, chance** – Unassignable cause due to random variation, usually due to materials, machines, or man.

**Celsius/Centigrade** – Temperature scale in which one degree is equivalent to 1/100 the difference between the temperature of melting ice and boiling water at standard atmospheric pressure.

**Cellophane** – Regenerated cellulose plastic packaging material.

**Cellulose** – Water soluble component of vegetable fiber.

**Chapetas** – Similar to whole wheat tortillas, but much larger in size.

**Champagne** – Sparkling wine produced from champagne region in France. Also carbonated wine.

**Characteristic** – Attributes or variables that distinguish products.

**Char cuterie** – Cold cuts or cold meat slices.

**Chateaubriand** – A thick slice of beef taken from the middle of the fillet which is grilled and served with garnished potatoes and other vegetables and accompanied by chateau sauce or bearnaise sauce.

**Chelating agent** – Chemical used to form stable complexes with metals.

**Chill** – To cool in a refrigerator but not freeze.

**Chi Square** – A statistic used to measure the discrepancy between a set of observed frequencies and their corresponding expected frequencies.

**Chloramine** – Anyone of various compounds containing nitrogen and chlorine.

**Chlorination** – To combine or treat with chlorine.

**Chlorine Demand** – difference between the amount of chlorine added to water and the total residual chlorine measured by the 5 minute orthotolidine test.

**Chlorine Dioxide** – A combination of chlorine and oxygen gases, prepared on site and used like chlorine as a sanitary agent.

**Cholesterol** – A fat soluble waxy substance found in animal cells.

**Cholestrol Levels** – 240 mg/desiliter of blood = "High Risk", 200-239 = "Borderline", below 200 = "Desirable".

**Chop** – To cut into small pieces with chopper or sharp knife.

**Chowder** – A thick soup, usually made with seafood and milk.

**Chroma** – One of the three terms used in the Munsell notations to denote color, referring to the amount of saturation or purity of the color.

**Chutney** – A condiment of acid foods usually made with raisins, dates, and onions.

**Clarification** – Purification of a liquid by removing the solid suspended particles.

**Class** – Designates a level or rank of quality (see Grade).

*Clostridium botulinum* — Bacteria that produce toxin responsible for food poisoning known as botulism. An anaerobic bacteria which produce very heat resistant spores. The organism is a gram-positive rod.

*Clostridium perfringens* – An anaerobic microorganism that causes food poisoning, with some spores very heat resistant. The organism is universally prevalent.

**Coagulant** – A substance which when added to liquids to form insoluble floc particles that absorb and precipitate colloidal and suspended solids.

**Coagulate** – To thicken or congeal.

**Coat** – To cover with a thin layer of flour, sugar, nuts, crumbs, Sesame or Poppy seed, Cinnamon sugar or a few of the ground spices.

**Coddle** – To cook slowly and gently just below the simmering point, as eggs and fruit.

**Codex Alimentarius** – International food standards.

**Coefficient of Variability (CV)** – A measure of variation of observations that has been adjusted for sample magnitude so that variation between samples with different magnitude can be compared. It may be calculated by dividing the Standard Deviation by the Average times 100. Thus, the CV value is reported in percent.

**Cohesive** – Gummy, rubbery texture of starch-paste.

**Collagen** – Insoluble animal protein found in connective tissues. Collagen can be converted to gelatine with moist heat.

**Colloid** – Fine particles suspended in a liquid or solid.

**Color** – A characteristic of light, arising from the presence of light in greater intensities at some wave lengths than at others in that band of the electromagnetic spectrum from 380 to 770 nanometers, to which the human eye is sensitive. The term color includes black, white and intermediate grays.

**Colors** – Usually meaning artifical dyes permitted for use in foods (Blue No. 1 and 2, Green No. 3, Red No. 3 and 40, and yellow No. 5 and 6).

**Colorant–** Any substance that imparts color.

**Commercial Sterility** – Condition when equipment and containers are free of viable microorganism with public health significance as well as those of non-health significance capable of reproducing under normal conditions of storage and distribution.

**Complimentary Color** – That color, which combined with the color considered in the proper portion, yields an achromatic, or gray mixture.

**Compote** – Fruits cooked slowly in syrup (may be spiced), during which time they retain their shape. Also, refers to a steamed dish.

**Conched** – A term used to define the process of kneading chocolate in special heated mixing tanks provided with pressure rollers that grind and aerate the now melted mass to develop increased smoothness, viscosity, and flavor.

**Condiment** – Flavoring agent used to make food savory or spicy.

**Condition** – The degree of soundness of a product.

**Conduction heating** – Transfer of energy from one particle to another without displacing the particles.

**Confectionery** – A branch of cookery where sugars are transformed into sweets.

**Congeal** – To change from a liquid to a semi-solid, non-fluid mass.

**Consistency** – A measure of the apparent viscosity, firmness, or thickenss of a product.

**Consumme** – Meat stock which has been enriched, concentrated and clarified.

**Container** – A box or receptacle which is usually the outer protection used in packing consumer cans, jars, or plastic packages.

**Contaminate** – To soil, stain, or infect with filth.

**Control Chart** – A graphic presentation where one measured characteristic of a process is plotted over time. The control chart has a central line representing the average designated by X Bar, and Control Limits representing what the process can do when operating consistently. The Control Limits (Upper and Lower) are calculated statistically using actual data from the process.

**Controlled Atmosphere (CA) Storage** – A storage environment in which the temperature, oxygen, carbon dioxide and other gases are adjusted for optimum conditions for any given product.

**Convection heating** – Transfer of energy from one part to another via a gas, fluid, or liquid mixing with one portion or another.

**Cooking** – Preparation of food by exposure to heat, that is, baking, boiling, frying, microwaving, roasting, etc.

**Coquille** – Shell or shell dish for baking and serving foods.

**Correlation** – The relationship between two factors such as height and weight, or color and maturity. The correlation coefficient "r" is expressed as a decimal value ranging from $-1$

to +1. If "r" equals zero there is no correlation and values approaching 1 + or − indicate a near perfect relationship. Correlations less than 0.7 are generally not practically significant to draw positive conclusions about the relationships.

**Cousinette** – A soup made with spinach, sorrel, lettuce and other green herbs all of which are cut up very fine.

**Covariance** – Varying together.

**Cracklings** – The residue left from rendered pork fat that has had the lard extracted.

**Cream** – To make soft, smooth and creamy by rubbing with back of spoon or by beating with mixer; usually applied to fat and sugar.

**Creole** – Term applied to various culinary preparations which usually contain rice.

**Crepe** –A very thin pancake of French origin made with eggs and flour which is poured sparingly into a frying pan and fried on both sides.

**Crisp-tender** – Cooked until just tender, but not soft or limp.

**Croissant** – A rich crescant shaped roll.

**Croquette** – Finely chopped meat or fish combined with thick white sauce, frequently cone-shaped, coated with egg and crumbs and fried until crisp.

**Croutons** – Small toasted or fried cubes of bread, may be seasoned.

**Crude Fiber** – Cellulose and lignin; indigestible substances found in many food products.

**Cryogenics** – Very low temperature (-320 degree F.) freezing usually with liquid nitrogen.

**Crystallization** – The formation of crystals.

**Cube** – To cut into small pieces with 6 equal sides.

**Curing** – A food process used with pickling and certain types of meats.

**Curing agent** – Substances used to impart flavors and/or colors to food and to increase shelf-life of specific products like meats.

**Curry** – A combination of dry ground blend of many spices cooked slowly in butter and oil or sour milk before adding the fish, meat, eggs, or vegetables that are to be curried.

**Custard** – A cooked or baked sweetened mixture of milk and eggs.

**Cut** – To divide a food using a knife or scissors.

**Cut in** – To incorporate solid fat in dry ingredients until finely divided by using a cutting motion with two knives or a chopping motion with a pastry blender.

**Cyclamate** – Synthetic, non nutritive sweetner that is 25 times sweeter than sucrose (discovered in 1937).

# D

**Deaeration** - The removal of oxygen from food products.

**Decompose** - To break down a product, usually by decay or rot.

**Deep fat fry** - To fry food in enough fat to cover.

**Defect** - Any nonconformance of a unit of product from specified requirements of a single quality characteristics. Defects are classed as "minor", "major", "severe", or "critical" depending upon the severity and undesirability of the defect.

**Defective** - A unit of a product that has one or more defects.

**Degradation** - Chemical breakdown of foods.

**Dehydration** - The removal of water from food by heat.

**Dehydrofrozen** - A partially dryed product held in frozen form.

**Delamination** - A separation of the laminate materials.

**Deleterious** - Harmful or hurtful substance, non-chemical.

**Demersal fish** - Near bottom of sea and on continental shelves, such as, cod, haddock, whiting, flounder, halibut, perch, shrimp, oysters, clams and crabs.

**Demi-tasse** - Very small cup of black coffee.

**Deordization** - Removal or stripping away of volatile trace compounds from oil by injecting high temperature steam (400-500 degree F) into the oil while under 7 or more mm of Mercury.

**Dependent Variable** – That variable for which a solution is sought, from a knowledge of the value of one or more correlated independent variables.

**Dessert** – The last course of a meal, may be cheese, fruits or sweets.

**Deterioration** – Advanced changes concerning the quality of foods.

**Detergent** – A cleansing agent, generally a surface active organic compound that emulsifies the "dirt" and lowers the surface tension of the water.

**Deviant** – A sample unit affected by one or more deviations or one that varies in a specially defined manner from the requirements of a standard, specification or other inspection document.

**Deviation** – Any specifically defined variation from a particular requirement.

**Dextrose (glucose)** – A 6 carbon simple sugar. It is, also, a reducing sugar.

**Dew point** – The temperature at which vapor begins to condense.

**Dice** – To cut food into small cubes.

**Diet** – To eat or cause to eat less or eating according to a prescribed rule.

**Dietary Fiber** – Undigested carbohydrates including hemicellulose, pectic substances, gums, and other carbohydrates including cellulose and lignin.

**Dietetic Foods** – foods that are modified and intended to prevent or cure certain physiological conditions.

**Difference Test** – A test of food product quality without indicating any preference.

**Digest** – Converting food into a form so that it can be absorbed by the body.

**Direct Heating** – A means of heating a product involving direct contact between the heating medium (steam) and the product.

**Disaccharide** – A 12 carbon sugar.

**Disinfectant** – Generally a chemical used to kill vegetative microorganisms.

**Distillation** – the separation of liquid materials by heating the materials to their boiling point and condensing the resulting vapors.

**Drained Weight** – A measure of the weight of product after draining off the liquid portion or packing medium of that product in a given size of container.

**Dryness** – Little or no sugar, opposite of sweetness.

**Du jour** – Literally means "of the day" and generally refers to a given menu item of the day.

**Duo-trio** – A method of difference testing, that is, one of a pair of samples is identified and presented first. Then the observer receives two more samples as unknowns in random order. The observers task is to pick the different sample.

**Duplicates** – Results from units of experiments made under the same conditions.

**Dust** – To sprinkle or coat food lightly with flour or sugar.

**Dough** – A mixture of flour and other ingredients stiff enough to knead or roll.

**Dud** – A container with no vacuum.

**Dud Detector** – A mechanism designed to identify low vacuum containers and reject them.

**Duo-Trio** – A method of difference testing. One of a pair of samples is identified and presented to a judge (observer), then the judge receives two more samples as unknowns in random order and their task is to pick the different sample.

# E

**E'clair** – A small pastry filled with cream flavored with vanilla, coffee, or chocolate or iced with fondant icing.

**Effluent** – Waste water or other liquid, partially or completely treated or untreated flowing out of a processing operation or treatment plant.

**Elasticity** – The ability of a food to return to its original shape or size after it has been stressed.

**Emulsion** – A mixture of two mutually insoluble liquids in which one is dispersed in droplets throughout the other, that is, the dispersion of oil or fat particles in water.

**Enrichment** – Improving the quality of a food up to a specified nutritional standard by adding nutrients to the original food.

**Enology** – The art, science and study of Wine making.

**Enrobe** – To coat a product, generally by dipping.

**Enterotoxin** – A toxin specific for cells of the intestine which may give rise to symptoms of food poisoning.

**Entree** – The principal dish of a meal in the US.

**Enzymatic Browning** – The darkening of plant tissues by chemical action caused by enzyme activity.

**Enzyme** – A complex mostly protein product of living cells that induces or speeds chemical reactions in plants and animals (man) without being itself permanently altered.

**Essential Elements** – Those elements necessary to maintain normal metabolic functions. Some are required to trace quantities (iron, copper, and zinc) while others are required in larger amounts (calcium and magnesium).

**Essential oils** – Natural oils that have been isolated and concentrated for use as in perfumes, foods, and beverages.

**Ester** – An alcohol with one or more fatty acids attached.

**Estouffade** – A dish whose ingredients are slowly stewed.

**Eutectic Point** – Temperature at which a substance exists simultaneously in the solid, liquid, and gaseous states.

**Evaporate** – to drive out the moisture within a product.

**Exhaust** – To remove or draw out air or gases from a can, jar, or package prior to closure.

**Extract** – An alcohol or alcohol-water solution containing a flavoring agent.

**Extrude** – To force, press, or punch out through a die.

# F

**F value** – Defined as number of minutes required to destroy a stated number of microorganisms at a defined temperature, usually at 250 degree F.

**Factorial experiment** – An experiment in which the treatments are arranged in all possible combinations.

**Facultative Anaerobes** – Microorganisms which can be grown either in the presence or absence of oxygen.

**Facultative Bacteria** – Bacteria which can exist and reproduce under either aerobic or anaerobic conditions.

**Fahrenheit** – A measure of temperature with water freezing at 32 and boiling at 212 degree F.

**Farina** – Refined cereal that is made from wheat that has been ground and sifted.

**Farinograph** – An instrument used to determine the quality of hard wheat flour, primarily measuring the protein quantity.

**Fat** – An ester of glycerol and a fatty acid. Natural fats are mixtures of various glycerides and at ambient temperatures are solid in form.

**Fatty Acid** – A chemical unit occurring naturally in plants or animals.

**Fermentation** – Decomposition of sugars to carbon dioxide and alcohol.

**Fertilizer** – Material used to enrich the land.

**Fiber** – A thread like crystalline substance found in both plants and animals and gives strength to the tissues.

**Fill Temperature** – The temperature of product at the time the container is filled.

**Fill Weight (Put-in-Weight)** – The amount of product put into a container prior to processing. It does not include the brine or liquid or the weight of the container.

**Fillet** – A piece or slice of boneless meat or fish.

**Fining** – the application of specific agents (tannins, gelatin, etc.) to clarify and stablize wines.

**Fire Point** – The temperature at which an oil will take fire and burn.

**Firming Agent** – Substances used to aid the coagulation of certain cheeses and to improve the texture of processed fruits and vegetables which might otherwise become soft.

**Fish Protein Concentrate** – Products prepared from whole edible fish.

**Flacid** – Deficient in firmness.

**Flambe** – To set fire with brandy, rum, or other liqueur with high alcohol content just before serving the food.

**Flash Point** – The temperature at which an oil will flash when a flame is passed over the surface of the oil.

**Flat Sour** – Canned foods that have spoiled due to thermophillic or thermoduric microorganisms.

**Flavedo** – The outer colored portion or peel of an orange.

**Flavor** – An attribute of foods, beverages, and seasonings resulting from the stimulation of taste and odor senses. A common term to describe the sensation aroused by taste testing a product.

**Flavoring agents** – Substances added to foods to enhance or change their taste.

**Flavor Profile** – A method of defining flavor in terms of characteristic notes or after taste effects.

**Flexible Packages** – Containers, usually made from laminated plastic materials, which bend and change shapes depending on internal and external pressures.

**Flocculation** – The process of forming larger masses from a large number of finer suspended particles.

**Florentine (la)** – A method of preparation of food used mainly for fish and eggs that are set in a bed of spinach and stewed in butter and covered with mornay sauce and sprinkled with cheese prior to serving.

**Flow Chart** – Step by step depiction of the unit operations in the processing of a food product.

**Flower crops as foods** – Artichoke, Broccoli and Cauliflower.

**Fluming** – Water conveyance of food or other materials.

**Fluoridation** – Addition of fluorides to water.

$F_o$– Time in minutes to destroy a given number of microorganisms of a reference strain at a temperature of 250 °F when the Z value is equal to 18 °F.

**Fold in** – A gentle and careful combining of a light or delicate mixture with a heavier mixture.

**Fondant** – An aqueous solution of invert sugar and corn syrup.

**Fondue** – A hot cheese dip.

**Food analog** – Fabricated food that resembles an animal or plant product.

**Food** – Articles used for food or drink for man or other animals, chewing gum, and articles used for components of any such article (FDA). Material taken into an organism and used for growth, repair, and vital processes and as source of energy.

**Food Chemical Codex** – A set of standards for purity of food chemicals in terms of maximum allowable trace contaminants, and methods of analysis for the contaminants.

**Food Infection** – An illness caused by an infection produced by invasion, growth and damage to the tissues of the host due to the ingestion of viable pathogenic microorganisms associated with the food.

**Food Intoxication** – An illness resulting from the ingestion of bacterial toxin with or without viable cells. The illness does not require actual growth of cells in the intestinal tract.

**Food Poisoning** – A general term applied to all stomach or intestinal disturbances due to food contaminated with certain microorganisms or their toxins.

**Food Science and Technology** – The field of study concerned with the application of science and technology to the processing, preservation, packaging, distribution, and utilization of foods and food products.

**Form-Fill & Seal** – Packaging equipment which forms containers from roll stock or body blanks, fills the product into the container, followed by sealing the container.

**Fortified food** – A food that specific nutrients have been added to like iron added to wheat flour.

**Fragrant** – A pleasing olfactory quality.

**Free Fatty Acids** – The released fatty acids from a monoglyceride, diglyceride or triglyceride. The amount of free fatty acids in an oil is a measure of its quality.

**Free Residual Chlorine** – The amount of uncombined chlorine in the water as measured by the 5 second orthotolidine test.

**Freeze Dry** – A process of food preservation wherein the original product is frozen and the water removed while the product is in the frozen condition. The finally dried product is then shelf-stable.

**Freezer Burn** – Drying out of food, generally due to inadequate wrapping.

**Freezing Point** – Temperature at which a liquid becomes solid.

**Fricasse** – A dish made of cut-up meats and cooked in a white sauce.

**Fritter** – A deep fried dough, usually containing fruits or meats.

**Frozen Foods** – Foods that are preserved by quick freezing and held at 0 degree F or below until ready for use.

**Fructose (Levulose)** – A very sweet six carbon reducing sugar found naturally in nature (Honey and Fruits).

**Fruit crops** – Apples, peaches, pears, strawberries, etc. and vegetables include cucumbers, eggplant, melons, peppers, pumkin and squash, and tomatoes.

**Fry** – To cook uncovered in fat by cooking in a pan or by immersing food in hot fat and cooking.

**Fudge** –A soft creamy candy consisting of milk, sugar, butter and flavorings.

**Fumigation** – Destruction of pests by exposure to fumes of gases.

**Fungi** – Plants which contain no chlorophyll, that is, molds.

**Fungicide** – An agent that controls or kills fungi.

# G

**Galactose** – A six carbon sugar obtained by hydrolysis of lactose.

**Garbage** – Food waste.

**Garnish** – To add decorative or savory touches to food.

**Gasket** – Pliable material between cover and container sealing surface designed to maintain a hermetic seal.

**Gastronomy** – The act and appreciation of good food.

**Gel** – To frim, semirigid-textured, colored starch-paste resembling a jelly, or to form a gel.

**Gelatinize** – The formation of a viscous gel.

*Geotrichum* – The name of a mold which can grow on food machinery.

**Germicide** – Chemical agent that will kill micro-organisms.

**Glass Container** – Containers made by melting sand and other materials and used for preservation of food. Glass containers are generally made from molds. There are three parts to most glass containers used by the food industry:
    **Finish** - Its that part of the container for holding the cap or closure. In the manufacturing process, it is made in the neck ring of the finish ring. The finish has several specfic areas as follows:
        Sealing – That portion of the finish which makes contact with the sealing gasket or liner. The sealing surface may be on the top of the finish, the side of the finish, or may be a combination of both top and side seal.
        Glass Lug – One of several horizontal tapering protruding ridges of glass around the periphery of the finish that permit specially designed edges or lugs on the closure

**Glass Container —** Continued

to slide between these protrusions and fasten the closure securely with a partial turn.

Continuous Thread – A continuous spiral projecting glass ridge on the finish of a container intended to mesh with the thread of a screw-type closure.

**Body** –It is that part of the container which is made in the "body-mold" and it is the largest part of the continer.

The charactertistic parts of the body of a glass container areas follows:

Shoulder – That portion of a glass container in which the maximum cross-section or body area decreases to join the neck or finish area.

Heel – The heel is the curved portion between the bottom and the beginning of the straight area of the side wall.

Side Wall – The area between the Shoulder and the Heel.

Mold Seam – A vertical mark on the glass surface in the body area resulting from matching the two parts of the body wall.

**Bottom or Bearing Surface** – That portion of the container in which it rests.

**Glassine** – A type of paper characterized by long wood pulp fibers which impart physical strength to the paper.

**Glaze** – To brown under the broiler a white sauce poured over cooked eggs, fish, chicken, etc. or to coat food with a glossy clear substance such as a gelatine, pureed fruit, jam, etc.

**Glossy** – Having a surface of luster or brightness.

**Glucose (dextrose)** – A 6 carbon sugar found widely in nature and 74% as sweet as sucrose.

**Glutamate** – Flavor enhancer.

**Gluten** – Protein from the endosperm of wheat.

**Glyceride –** Organic compounds resulting from the reaction of fatty acid and glycerol.

**Glycolipid –** A class of compounds in which a carbohydrate is combined with a lipid.

**Glycoprotein –** A class of compounds in which a carbohydrate is combined with a protein.

**Goulash –** A beef stew made with onions, paprika, and carraway.

**Gourmet –** One who is accustomed to or connoisseur of the best of foods.

**Grade –** To classify foods into different categories based on their quality characteristics or attributes, such as,

Grade A (Fancy) – Excellent high quality foods, practically uniform in size and very symmetrical, practically free of any defects, uniform in color, excellent in respect to texture, and color.

Grade B (Choice term for fruits and Extra Standard term for Vegetables) – High quality foods, reasonably uniform in size, good color texture and reasonably free from defects.

Grade C  (Standard Quality) – Fairly good to good quality foods, fairly uniform in size, color and texture. Fairly free from defects.

Grade D (Sub Standard Quality) – Products which fail to meet the requirements of Grade C level of quality or the Minimum Standard of Quality as designated by the Food and Drug Administration.

**Grate –** To cut into minute particles by rubbing over a grater.

**Grilling –** A method of cooking food by putting it on a grill or under a broiler.

**Grind –** To crush to small particles by putting through a grinder or by putting through a mill with a sharp blade or by reducing in size as in a food processor.

**Grits** - Broken cereal grains, mostly white corn.

**Guar Gum** - A stabilizer, thickener, and emulsifier.

**Gum** - Class of water soluble colloidal substances that are exuded by plants.

**Gumbo** - A rich thick soup usually thickened with okra.

**Gumming** - Formation and accumulation of a fat insoluble sticky material resulting from continued heating of oils. It is produced by oxidation and polymerization of the oil and represents oil breakdown products which collect on the heating surfaces.

**Gustatory** - The sensation of taste.

# H

**Halophillic** – Descriptive of microorganisms that will grow only if a very high salt concentration is present; salt loving.

**Hardness** – A measure (in ppm) of the presence of calcium, magnesium, etc. in water which form insoluble precipitates with soap.

**Hash** – Chopped meat mixed with potatoes and browned.

**Headspace** – The non-filled volume of a container (up to 10% of the capacity of the container) which allows for product expansion.

**Hedonic Scale** – A scale from 1 to 9 used for the evaluation of foods with a degree of liking from 1 to 5 and degree of disliking from 5 to 9.

**Heat, Latent** – Heat absobed or liberated in a change of physical state such as evaporation, condensation, freezing or sublimation· expressed as BTU per lb.

**Heat, Sensible** – Heat that has gone into raising the temperature of steam without change of pressure or absolute humidity.

**Herb** – Aromatic leaves and sometimes the flowers of plants, usually of temperate origin.

**Herbicide** – An agent used to destroy unwanted plants.

**Hermetic** – Air tight seal.

**Hermeticlly Sealed Container** – container designed to become secure against the entry of microorganisms and to maintain commercial sterility of its content.

**Hexose** – A six carbon sugar.

**Hibachi** – A charcoal grill.

**Histogram** – A bar diagram representing a frequency distribution of a particular attribute that is measured in the process or of a product.

**Hollandaise** – The name of a hot sauce made with yolks of eggs and butter and served with eggs, fish or vegetables.

**Homogenization** – The process of making incompatible or immiscible components into a stabilized uniform suspension in a liquid form.

**Hops** – A plant whose flowers contain resins and essential oils that contribute to the characteristic bitter flavor and pleasant aroma of beer.

**Hors d'oeuvre** – Colorful and attractive and savory foods or relishes usually served as appetizers.

**Horsepower** – A measure of heat, energy or work.

**Hue** – The attribute of color which is noted by such terms as blue, yellow, red, etc. A part of the Munsell system of color notation.

**Humectant** – A substance that is used to help maintain moisture in foods.

**Humidity** – The amount of moisture in the air.

**Hunger** – The strong desire or a craving for food.

**Hydrocolloids** – Water soluble gums.

**Hydrogenation** – A process employed to alter the chemical and physical properties of a fat or oil. Generally, hydrogenation is used to change a liquid oil into a semisolid or solid fat at ambient temperature and to enhance oxidative stability. The process involves the addition of hydrogen atoms to the carbon-to-carbon double bounds in unsaturated fatty acids. When oils are hydrogenated to saturation, the resulting products are hard, brittle white solids at room temperature with relatively high melting points.

**Hydrolysis–** A chemical reaction involving molecular breakdown by reaction with water forming acid or base or both.

**Hydrometer –** A floating device used to determine the specific gravity or density of liquids.

**Hydrophobic –** Water repellant; opposite of hydrophillic.

**Hydroponics –** Plant culture in nutrient aqueous solutions.

**Hydrostatic Retort –** A still retort in which pressure is maintained by a water leg; it operates at a constant steam temperature while containers are continuously conveyed through it for the required process times.

**Hygiene –** A science dealing with the establishment and maintenance of health.

**Hygrometer –** An instrument for measuring relative humidity or the available water.

**Hygroscopic –** The absorption of moisture from water vapor.

**Hypha –** Fungal filament.

**Hypochlorites –** Combination of chlorine with either sodium or calcium hydroxide to give a desired available chlorine.

# I

**Ice** – Frozen mixture of sugar or sugar syrup, fruit puree or flavoring and water.

**Icings (Frostings)** – A preparation made with sugar, egg whites and colorings for covering cakes.

**Incubation** – Maintenance of a food product at a specified temperature for a specific time to encourage the growth of microorganisms that may be present in the sample.

**Independent Variable** – A variable which on the basis of a previously established relationship with a dependent variable, may be used for the solution of specific values of the dependent variable.

**Indirect Heating** – A means of heating a product in which the product and heating medium are physically separate.

**Indigestible** – Food that is not readily digested.

**Initial temperature (IT)** – The average temperature of the contents of the coldest container to be processed at the time the sterilizing cycle begins, as determined after thorough stirring or shaking of the filled and sealed container.

**Inoculate** – The artificial introduction of microorganisms into a system.

**Inoculum** – The material containing microorganisms used for inoculation.

**In-plant chlorination** – Chlorination beyond the break point of water used in a food plant, usually to a residual of 5 to 7 ppm.

**Insecticide** – A chemical agent used to destroy insects either by contact or by stomach poisoning.

**Insoluble Fibers** – Cellulose, hemicellulose and lignin materials that stimulate intestines, accelerate food transit time and increases weight and softness of the stool.

**Instant** – Partially prepared foods by the manufacturer to make food preparation easier.

**Interaction** – The tendency for the combination of two factors to produce a result that is different from the mere sum of the two individual contributions.

**Interstate** – Between the states.

**Intoxication** – The adverse physiological effects of an organism of consuming a toxic substance.

**Intrastate** – Within a state.

**Invertase** – An enzyme that hydrolyzes sucrose to glucose and fructose.

**Invert sugar** – Sugar formed by acid hydrolysis of fructose and glucose.

**Iodine Value** – A measure of the degree of unsaturation of a fat or oil, it refers to the number of grams of iodine absorbed by 100 gm of fat.

**Iodized salt** – Table salt to which 0.1% sodium or potassium iodide has been added.

**Iodophors** – A combination of iodine with a wetting agent which slowly releases free iodine in the water.

**Ion** – A charged particle.

**Ion Exchange** – A reversible chemical reaction between a solid and a liquid by means of which ions may be interchanged between the two. It is in common use in water softening and water deionizing.

**Irradiation** – Sterilization utilizing high-energy electro-magnetic radiation.

**Isoelectric point** – Each protein has a point at which it can become either an acid or alkaline, that is, the neutral or isolelectric point. At this point the protein is least soluble and will precipitate out of solution.

# J

**Jams –** A viscous or semi-solid food made with 45 parts by weight of saccharine ingredient. Spices, acidifying agents, pectin, buffering agents, preservatives, and antifoaming agents, except those derived from animal sources may be added.

**Jardiniere –** Assortment of fresh vegetable in fancy shapes used to garnish a main course.

**Jelly –** A jellied food made with a mixture of strained fruit(s) (45 parts by weight) and 55 parts by weight of a saccharine ingredient. Spices, acidifying agents, pectin, buffering agents, preservatives and antifoaming agents except those derived from animal sources, and mint flavoring or cinnamon flavoring may be added.

**Jeroboam –** Double magnum.

**Jus –** An extract from meat.

**Judge –** An observer or person trained to observe and record his or her findings.

**Julienne –** To cut foods into 2 to 3 inch long strips by 1/8 inch wide.

# K

**Kebob –** Cubes of meat cooked with vegetables usually on a skewer.

**Kinesthetics –** Refers to a sense of feel by the mouth or fingers.

**Kneading –** To work or press into a mass with the heel of the hands while stretching and folding the dough.

**Kilowatt –** A unit of electric power equal to 1000 watts.

**Kurtosis –** Degree of peakedness.

**Kwashiorkor –** An acute form of protein-calorie malnutrition.

# L

**Label –** A display of written, printed, or graphic matter upon the immediate container of any article; and a requirement made by or under authority of the Federal Food, Drug, and Cosmetic Act that any word, statement, or other information appear on the label shall not be considered to be complied with unless such word, statement, or other information also appears on the outside container or wrapper, if any there be, of the retail package of such article, or is easily legible through the outside container of the wrapper. The label in addition to other things, must state the true name of the product, a list of ingredients in descending order, the name and business place of the manufacturer, packer, or distributor; and an accurate statement of the quantity of the contents in terms of weight, measure, or numerical count.

**Lactose –** A 12 carbon disaccharide milk sugar derived from whey.

**Lagoon –** A large pond of water used to hold wastewater for stabilization by natural processes.

**Lasagne –** Italian pasta cut in the shape of wide ribbons used with ground beef and cheeses and baked.

**Latent Heat –** The quantity of heat, measured in BTU's or calories, necessary to change the physical state of a substance without changing its temperature, such as in distillation.

**Leaf crops –** Cabbage, collards, endive, kale, lettuce, parsley, spinach, watercress, etc.

**Leaven –** A substance (yeast) used to produce fermentation (dough).

**Lees –** Sediment at the bottom of a fermentation tank.

**Legumes –** Beans, peas, lentils and peanuts as examples.

**Linoleic acid** – An essential fatty acid not synthesized by the body and therefore must be obtained from the diet.

**Lipid** – A general term for fats and oils.

**Liqueur** – A mixture of spirits and syrups.

**Liquify** – To reduce to a liquid.

**Lot** – Any number of containers of the same size and type which contain a product of the same type and style located in the same warehouse or conveyance, or which, under in-plant (in-process) inspection, results from consecutive production within a plant, and which is available for inspection at any one time.

**Low Acid Food** – Any foods, other than alcoholic beverages, with a finished equilibrium pH greater than 4.6 and a water activity greater than 0.85.

**Low calorie foods** – Food that contains less than 40 calories or 0.4 calories per gram.

**Low sodium foods** – Foods containing less than 140 mgs of sodium.

**Lower Control Limits of the Average** – A system of determining the pattern that sample averages should follow if a constant system of change is operating.

**Lycopene** – A red pigment found in tomatoes, watermelons, etc.

**Lye** – A strong alkaline solution, usually Caustic Soda (sodium hydroxide).

**Lyonnaise** – Cooked in a style of food prepared in a region of France famed for excellent onions.

# M

**Macaroon** – A small round dry pastry made of almond paste, sugar and the white of an egg.

**Macaroni** – A nourishing product made from wheat flour (semolina, durum, farina), and water or milk and eggs and dried into tubes.

**Macronutrients** – Nutrients which are required in relatively large amounts by humans to maintain normal growth and other body functions.

**Magnum** – Double size wine bottle (48 to 56 fluid ounces).

**Maillard Reaction** – A dark color to certain foods resulting from the chemical interactions between sugars and proteins.

**Maitre d'hotel** – Head of the dining room.

**Malnourished** – Poorly nourished.

**Malnutrition** – Inadequate supply of nutrients.

**Marinade** – Liquid in which food is marinated, usually containing vegetables, spices, vinegar, wine, water, etc.

**Marinate** – To steep a food in a marinade to modify its flavor.

**Maltose** – A 12 carbon disaccharide sugar made up of two molecules of glucose and occurring in starch and glycogen.

**Mariculture** – Fish farming.

**Mash** – Term used in brewing to indicate the slow heating of a mixture of cereal grains and water to extract the soluble materials and gelatinize the starch to sugars.

**Maturation** - The phenomena of ripening in plants.

**Mean (Average) (X Bar)** - Defined as the quotient obtained by dividing the sum of a set of readings or observations by the number of observations.

**Mean Square** - An estimate of the population variance.

**Median** - This is the reading or observation above or below which an equal number of observations fall.

**Melba** - A crisp, thin, crunchy toast.

**Melt** - To dissolve or liquify by heating.

**Meringue** - A mixture of sugar and egg whites formed into small cakes and baked or spread over pastry etc.

**Mesophillic Bacteria** - Medium temperature loving bacteria that may grow readily at warehouse, store, or home conditions.

**Meuniere** - Fish dipped in flour and sauteed in butter.

**Microencapsulation** - The process of forming a thin protective coating around a particle of a substance.

**Micron** - One thousandth of a millimeter.

**Microorganism** - Living cells seen only with the aid of a powerful microscope. A general term referring to bacteria, molds and yeasts.

**Microwave Cooking** - A method of cooking food by the heat produced as a result of microwave penetration of the food in a microwave oven. Microwaves are high-frequency electromagnetic energy (300 to 30,000 megaHertz).

**Mince** - To cut or chop into small pieces.

**Minestrome** - A thick rich vegetable soup.

**Mix** - To combine all ingredients evenly.

**Mode** - The value that occurs most frequently in a set of data.

**Mornay Sauce** – A white sauce flavored with cheese and thickened with egg yolks.

**Moisture** – Usually referred to as the water content of the food.

**Molds** – Multi celled, microscopic organisms which usually reproduce from spores. Often called fungi.

**Molecular Weight** – Sum of the atomic weights of all the atoms in a molecule.

**Molecule** – The smallest theoretical quantity of a material that retains the properties exhibited by the material.

**Monosaccharide** – A six carbon sugar

**Mousse** – A frozen whipped cream to which sugar, flavor and ice cream mix have been added or a molded chilled dessert made with sweetened and flavored whipped cream or egg whites and gelatin.

**Mouthfeel** – A description of a food based on its viscosity and or consistency.

**Muffin** – A small soft biscuit baked in a cup shaped container.

**Muffuletta** – A monumental sandwich creation which boasts an unusual combination of ingredients including olive salad layered between halves of chewy Italian bread loaves.

**Mulligatawny** – Thick soup of Indian origin with curry.

**Must** – Crushed fruit or juice ready for fermentation.

**Mycelium** – A microscopic thread like filament, a part of the mold.

**Mycotoxin** – A poisonous compound produced by molds.

**Mylar** – A polyester resin used in food packaging.

# N

**Nacho** – A very hot spicy condiment or flavoring.

**Natural Foods** – Term describing foods which are grown without chemical fertilizers or pesticides. Also, foods in the preparation of which no synthetic preservatives are used.

**Nectar** – A fruit puree (crushed fruits with seeds removed) that may or may not be sweetened and with or without the addition of water for consistency control.

**Net Weight** – The weight of the product in the container exclusive of the container.

**Neutralize** – To adjust the pH of a solution to 7.0 (neutral) by the addition of an acid or base.

**Newburg Sauce** – Sauce of cream, sherry and egg yolks frequently combined with lobster and other shellfish.

**Newtonian** – Refers to the flow of liquids. The viscosity of Newtonian liquids does not change with the rate of shear. Newtonian liquids are essentially chemically pure and physically homogeneous.

**Non-Newtonian** – Materials whose flow characteristics change with the rate of shear. Non-Newtonian liquids are usually mixtures which are not chemically pure or physically homogeneous.

**Nicose** – A kind of salad made with potatoes and green beans, seasoned with oil, vinegar, salt and pepper, and arranged in a dome dish or pasta shell, and decorated with anchovies and garnished with tomatoes and sprinkled with chervil and tarragon.

**Noodle** – A pasta product containing no eggs.

**Normal Solution** – A solution concentration containing one gram-equivalent of a substance per liter of the solution.

**Normal** - Unless otherwise states, refers to the property of being distributed in the form of a normal frequency distribution.

**Normal Curve** - The distribution of individual values with the average, median, and mode the same. Further, the standard deviation divides the range of the set of data into six equal parts.

**Normande (A la)** - A method of preparation used mostly for fish braised in white wine, especially sole.

**Nougat** - A sweet made with roasted almonds and honey.

**Nucleic acids** - A complex compound which on hydrolysis yields phosphoric acid, sugars, and one or more bases.

**Nucleoprotein** - A combination of proteins and nucleic acids.

**Nucleotides** - A molecule consisting of one molecule of phosphoric acid, one molecule of sugar and one molecule of a base.

**Nutrient** - Any substance that contributes to the growth and health of a living organism.

**Nutrition**- The act or process of nourishing.

**Nutritional Information Panel** - Appears on food labels to the right of the principal display panel. It provides information on the nutritional composition of the food.

**Objective** – Capable of being recorded by physical instruments, not dependent upon the observer.

**Odor** – A sensory reaction based on vapors inhaled through the nostrils.

**Off-flavors** – Disagreeable sensation.

**Oil** – An edible fat that is liquid under ambient conditions.

**Olfactory Receptors** – Nerve endings which may be stimulated by odors.

**Omlet** – Eggs beaten or stirred with milk or water, cooked without stirring until set and then folded over.

**Operating Characteristic Curve** – The curve that gives the probability of acceptance of a lot of merchandise on the basis of a specified sampling plan.

**Organic** – Carbon containing compounds.

**Organic Foods** – Foods grown without use of synthetic compounded fertilizers, pesticides, growth regulators, and/or livestock feed additives.

**Organoleptic** – Affecting or making an impression upon an organ. Sometimes used as a synonym for sensory when referring to examination of products by taste or smell.

**Oriental** – Term applied to the preparation of various ingredients (fish, eggs, vegetables) cooked with tomatoes, flavored with garlic and sometimes spiced with saffron.

**Osmophilic** – Organisms that can grow or survive in a medium very low in humidity or of low water activity level.

**Osmosis** – Diffusion between two miscible fluids separated by a permeable wall.

**Oxidation** – A chemical reaction involving the addition or combination of oxygen with another material.

**Oxygen Scavenger** – An antioxidant.

# P

**Packaging** – Placing food in containers (metal, glass, plastic) suitable for distribution and protection from bacterial contamination, moisture loss, oxidative deterioration.

**Pack Date** – Date of manufacturing, processing or packaging.

**Packing Medium** – The liquid or other medium in which the low acid or acidified products are packed.

**Palatable** – Agreeable to the taste; savory; hence acceptable or pleasing.

**Paired comparison** – A psychometric or psychophysical method in which samples are presented in pairs for comparison, on the basis of some definite criterion, such as preference, intensity, degree of a defined quality.

**Pallet** – A low, portable platform of wood, metal, fiberboard, or combination thereof, to facilitate handling, storage and transportation of materials as a unit.

**Palletizing** – The forming of a pallet load.

**Panel** – A group of people (observers, subjects, judges, panelists) comprising a test population which has been specially selected or designated in some manner, e.g. they may be trained, or have special knowledge of skills, or may merely be available and predesignated.

**Paneling** – Distortion (side wall collapses) of a container caused by the development of a reduced pressure (too high vacuum) inside the container.

**Panfry** – To cook, uncovered, with a small quantity of fat.

**Papain** – An enzyme found in the juice of unripe papayas.

**Par boil** – To cook partially in boiling salted water or other liquid.

**Parameter** – A numerical characteristic of a population, estimated by a statistic, such as, average, range, or standard deviation.

**Pare** – To peel or trim off outside covering as with peeling of many fruits and vegetables.

**Pareto Chart** – Ranking of all potential problems or data or sources of variations wherein the points are prioritized and the trivial many causes are separated from the vital few.

**Parfait** – Ice made of single flavored mousse mixture set in plain molds.

**Parmigiana** – Food covered with Parmesan cheese.

**Pasta** – A generic Italian term for many noodle like pastes or doughs (over 500 kinds), generally means a paste in processed form as in spaghetti or in the form of fresh dough as in ravioli.

**Pasteurization** – Mild heat treatment used to kill the vegetative forms of specific bacteria in liquid or semiliquid food products.

**Pastry** – A baked product made of flour, shortening and water and sometimes eggs and or milk may be used.

**Pate** – A meat or fish pie or patty; a spread of freshly mashed, seasoned meat or fish.

**Pathogenic** – Disease producing microorganisms.

**Pectin** – Water soluble substances found in plant tissues that may cause geling.

**Pelagic fish** – Middle and surface water fish, as mackerel, salmon, tuna, etc.

**Peptides –** Compounds of two or more amino acids linked by a peptide bond.

**Pericarp –** The plant material surrounding the seed of fruits.

**Permeability –** The passage or diffusion of a gas, vapor, liquid, or solid through a barrier without physically or chemically affecting it.

**Peroxidase –** Ubiquitous enzyme occuring in higher plants and leukocytes.

**Peroxide –** A compound containing a large amount of oxygen.

**Peroxide Value or Number –** A value indicating the amount of oxidation taken place in a given fat or oil based on the peroxides present in the oil.

**Pesticide –** Any substance which, alone, in chemical combination or in formulation with one or more other substances, is an "economic poison" within the meaning of the Federal Insecticide, Fungicide, and Rodenticide Act.

**Petits fours (Bouchees) –** Puffed pastry patties, baked, and filled with various compositions.

**pH –** Degree or intensity of acidity or alkalinity of a solution or of a product. Technically, it is the negative logarithm of the hydrogen ion concentration. pH is measured on a scale of 0-14 with 7 being neutral. 0-7 is acidic and 7-14 is basic, however, in the food industry 4.6 is neutral with food products less than 4.6 classed as acid foods and food with a pH of 4.6 or higher as low acid foods. Most foods have a pH below 7.0 (See Appendix Table).

**Relationship of pH Value To Concentration
of Acid (H+) of Alkalinity (OH−)**

| pH Value | Concentration | |
|---|---|---|
| 0 | 10,000,000 | |
| 1 | 1,000,000 | |
| 2 | 100,000 | |
| 3 | 10,000 | Acidity |
| 4 | 1,000 | |
| 5 | 100 | |
| 6 | 10 | |
| 7 | 0 | Neutral |
| 8 | 10 | |
| 9 | 100 | |
| 10 | 1,000 | |
| 11 | 10,000 | Alkalinity |
| 12 | 100,000 | |
| 13 | 1,000,000 | |
| 14 | 10,000,000 | |

**Pheophytin** – Compound formed by conversion of chlorophyll, that is, the formation of a green color to olive green or brown color.

**Phospholipids** – Emulsifying compounds made up primarily of lecithin found in yolk of eggs.

**Photosynthesis** – The formation of carbohydrates from carbon dioxide and water by chlorophyll containing plants exposed to sunshine.

**Pickling** – A method of food preservation using vinegar or salt brine.

**Pigment** – A colorant.

**Pilaf, Pilaff, Pilau, or Pilaw** – A dish of rice or cracked wheat.

**Piquant** – Food characterized by pleasantly pungent or sharp flavor.

**Pita bread (Often called pocket bread)** – Round flat bread usually made from whole wheat flour that can be opened at one end to form a pocket for stuffing with sandiwch fillings or salads.

**Pizza** – A baked crust covered with tomato paste or puree with or without diced tomatoes, cheese, and other toppings, such as, sausage (pepperoni), mushrooms, peppers, etc.

**Pliofilm** – Rubber hydrochloride film used in packaging.

**Plump** – To soak in liquid or moisten thoroughly and heat in 350 degree F. oven until full and round.

**Poach** – To cook in water just below the boiling point of the water.

**Polymerization** – An undesirable change in the composition of a fat or oil involving intermolecular agglomeration or clumping of the normal units of the fat or oil.

**Polysaccahride** – Carbohydrate compounds like starch, cellulose, and pectic substances.

**Polyunsaturated** – A fatty acid having more than one unsaturated bond.

**Pomace** – The residue left after pressing the juice from fruit products consisting of cores, seeds, and skins.

**Potable** – Pure enough to drink.

**Prawn** – Term used to describe a large shrimp.

**Preference** – Expression of a high degree of liking or the choice of one product over another.

**Preservation** – Physical or chemical processes which prevents or delays food spoilage or food deterioration.

**Precison** – Refers to the standard deviation, coefficient of variability, or relative precision. The smaller the value the greater the precision. The closer the agreement between duplicates, the higher the precision.

**Pretzel** – A savory biscuit, baked hard in the shape of a loose knot, sprinkled with salt and sometimes covered with cumin seeds.

**Principal Display Panel** – That part of a label on a food package that is most likely to be shown or examined under customary conditions of display for retail sales.

**Probability** – The relative frequency of objects or things in a given class of a probability set.

**Probability Distribution** – A distribution of relative frequencies.

**Process** – Application of heat to foods either before or after sealing in a container for a period of time and at a temperature scientifically determined to be adequate to achieve commercial sterility.

**Process Authority** – The person or organization that scientifically established thermal processes for low-acid canned foods or processing requirements for acidified foods.

**Process Calculation** – Mathematical procedure to determine the adequate proces time and temperature for thermally processed foods.

**Process Capability** – ($C_p$) – A value to serve as a guide as to how well the process is in control. Calculated by dividing the specification width (Upper Specification-Lower Specification) by the natural tolerance (6 sigma).

**Process Deviation** – A change in any critical factor of the scheduled process which reduces the sterilizing value of the process or which raises a question regarding the public health safety and or commercial sterility of the product lot.

**Process Schedule** – The process selected by the processor as adequate under the conditions of manufacture for a given product to achieve commercial sterility.

**Proof** – A measurement of alcohol strength; one degree of proof equals ½ of the percentage of alcohol (by volume).

**Propyl gallate** – An antioxidant.

**Propionates** – A food additive having the property of inhibiting the growth of molds.

**Protein** – A dietary source of amino acids and nitrogen required for growth, maintenance and general well being of humans.

**Provolone** – Hard cheese of Italian origin, rich, smoky and somewhat sharp flavor.

**Pseudoplastic** – Materials the viscosity of which decreases as the rate of shear to which the material is subjected increases.

**Psychrometer** – An instrument for measuring the humdidity (water-vapor) content of air.

**Psychrophillic Bacteria** – Bacteria that grow at low temperature (refrigerated temperatures).

**Pudding** – A dessert, usually baked or boiled. It is based on bread, rice, fruit together with milk, flour, sugar and flavoring.

**Pull Date** – The last day a retail store may offer an item for sale.

**Pulping** – Process of forcing food materials through a screen resulting in a puree.

**Puree** – A smooth paste, usually of vegetables or fruits, made by sieving, milling or beating in a blender.

**Putrefaction** – To make or become spoiled.

**Putrefactive** – Capable of breaking down protein causing a putrid odor.

# Q

**Qualitative factor** – A factor in which the different levels cannot be arranged in order of magnitude, such as, batches, methods, or materials produced in different plants.

**Quality** – That combination of attributes or characteristics of a product that have significance in determining the degree of acceptability of that product by the user.

**Quality Audit** – To verify or examine products or processes for compliance to specifications.

**Quality Assurance** – Processes and products are acceptable and in conformance to requirements.

**Quality Circle** – A group of people who meet together on a regular basis to identify, analyze, and solve quality and other problems in their area of work.

**Quality Control** – Regulation of processes and operations to some standard or specification; a tool for the production worker to control the unit operation and or line to some standard or specification.

**Quality Evaluation** – To describe or appraise the worth of a product according to some standard or specification, generally the taking of measurements of a product in a laboratory.

**Quiche** – A savory custard made with ham and/or other meats, vegetables, cheese, and eggs are baked in a pie crust and served hot.

**Quantitative factor** – Factors which can be arranged in order of magnitude, such as, temperature, pressure, velocities, pressures, or items measured on a numerical scale.

# R

**Racking** – The practice of syphoning wine from one container to another.

**Radiant Heating** – Transfer of energy from one body to another, not in contact with it, but by means of wave motion through space.

**Radicchio (Red Chicory)** – A salad green with wide uses. Known to cool foods, high in vitamin A and C and high in Calcium.

**Ragout** – A well seasoned meat, foul or fish stew.

**Ramekins** – Small oval or round individual baking dishes.

**Rancid** – A product having a rank odor or taste.

**Random Numbers** – Numbers from a table of random numbers used for sampling purposes.

**Random sample** – Samples that are taken in such a way that each member of the population or lot have an equal chance of being selected.

**Range** – Difference between upper and lower limit of a set of observations. It is one method of measuring the amount of variation.

**Rank** – The order of values of a sample.

**Ranking Test** – The arranging of food items in order of intensity.

**Ravioli** – Pasta stuffed with various mixtures and poached in salt water, moistened with beef gravy, and sprinkled with cheese.

**Recipe** – A set of instructions including a formula.

**Reconstitute** – To rehydrate (put moisture back into) dehydrated foods by soaking in a liquid (water).

**Reduce** – To boil liquid until part of the water is evaporated.

**Reduced calories** – less than one-third of the calories of the food it substitutes or resembles.

**Reduced sodium** – Reduction of usual level by 75%.

**Reducing Sugars** – A sugar which is easily oxidized, that is, glucose, fructose, maltose and lactose.

**Reduction** – A chemical reaction where hydrogen combines with another substance.

**Refractometer** – An optical instrument that measures the percent of soluble solids in solution by the extent to which a beam of light is bent (refracted). The soluble solids scale is based on sugar concentration in a pure sucrose solution.

**Rehoboam** – Triple magnum.

**Rehydrate** – To soak or cook dehydrated foods to restore their water content.

**Rejection Number** – The minimum number of deviants in a sample that will cause a lot to fail a specific requirement.

**Relative Humidity** – Ratio of water vapor present in the air to the quantity that would be present if the air were saturated at the same temperature.

**Relish** – A highly seasoned sauce eaten with other foods to add flavor to them.

**Render** – To free fat from animal tissue by heating at low temperatures.

**Replication** – A part of an experiment containing all the levels of all the factors once only. Sometimes called a block.

**Restaurant** –    A public establishment where food is served.

**Retort** – Any closed vessel or other equipment used for thermal processing.

**Retrogradation** – The reverse of gelatinization and hence dehydration and reversion of cooked starch from a paste to a condition of insolubility.

**Reuben** – A sandwich made with sauerkraut, ham and cheese and usually served on rye bread.

**Rheology** – The science treating of the deformation and flow of matter.

**Rice** – To force vegetables through a fine sieve or colander to break into small pieces.

**Roast** – to cook, uncovered, by dry heat in an oven or open spit.

**Rodent** – A knawing mammal, e.g., rat, mouse, squirrel.

**Rodenticide** – A poison used to kill rodents.

**Root crops** – Beets, carrots, parsnips, radish, rutabagas, salsify, and sweet potato.

**Roux** – A sauce made with flour and butter.

**Rotisserie** – A portable appliance designed to roast meat or a spit.

**Run Chart** – A graphic representation where one measured characteristic of a process is plotted over time.

# S

**Saccharin** - A non-nutritive sweetener 300 plus times as sweet as sucrose (discovered in 1879).

**Sake** - Rice wine.

**Salad** - A cold dish served with dressing.

**Salmonella** - Intestinal pathogenic bacteria that can exist at low temperature.

**Salometer** - A floating instrument used to test the strength or salinity of a salt or brine solution.

**Salt** - A white crystalline substance that consists of sodium (39%) and Chlorine (61%) and is used to season foods.
Sodium Free– Less than 5 mg per serving.
Very Low Sodium– 35 mg or less per serving.
Reduced Sodium– Reduction of usual level by 75%.

**Salty** - A quality of taste senation of which the taste of sodium chloride is the typical example.

**Sample** - A representative set of products ordinarily selected at random from a larger set called a lot and used for inspection or evaluation.

**Sample Unit** - A container and/or its entire contents, a portion of the contents of a container or other unit of commodity, or a composite mixture of a product to be used for inspection.

**Sampling** - The act or practice of selecting samples from a lot for the purpose of inspection.

**Sanitary** - Free from filth or infective matter.

**Sanitation** - Practice of protective measures for cleanliness and health.

**Sanitizer** - A cleaning chemical.

**Saponification** – The hydrolysis of mono-, di-, or triglycerides with caustic or alkali to form free glycerol and fatty acids in the form of soaps.

**Saran** – Polyvinylidene chloride, a plastic film for wrapping foods.

**Satiety** – The absence of a desire for food.

**Saturation** – Each atom of carbon capable of linking to other atoms by means of four covalent bonds.

**Sauce** – A liquid mixture or dressing for salads, meats, poultry, fish, and deserts to alter the flavor.

**Sausage** – Chopped  meat packed into casings.

**Saute** – To fry lightly or brown in a little oil or fat.

**Sauerbraten** – Beef soaked in water, vinegar, onion, salt, pepper, and bay leaves; cooked with soaking liquid and sour cream.

**Savor** – The taste or odor of something.

**Scald** – To heat food just below boiling point.

**Scale** – A standard set of values used to evaluate food products.

**Schaal Test** – A method for detection of onset of rancidity in fats or oils or food products.

**Schnitzle** – Thin cutlet of veal, coated with egg and breaded and then cooked in butter or oil.

**Score** – To rate the properties of a food product on a scale according to some standard or specification.

**Scrapple** – Sausage consisting of ground boneless pork and pork by-products, corn meal or flour, and seasoning.

**Sear** – To brown surface quickly over high heat in hot skillet or similar utensil or over a hot grill.

**Season** – To add salt, spices and other flavoring elements to food.

**Seasoning –** To make pleasant to the taste by the addition of salt, pepper, and or spices.

**Sedimentation –** The falling or settling of solid particles in a liquid, as a sediment.

**Seed crops –** Beans, peas, lentils, corn, wheat, rice, etc.

**Sensory –** Examination by smelling, feeling, tasting and/or seeing (appearance).

**Sequestrants –** Organic and inorganic compounds capable of forming complexes (chelating) with metals.

**Serving –** A portion of a food sufficient for one person.

**Sewage –** Waste, matter, or refuse carried off by sewers.

**Sewerage –** A system of sewers.

**Shall –** A mandatory requirement (FDA).

**Sharp –** An intense or painful reaction to a product, e.g., acids or alcohols.

**Shelf Life –** The storage time of a product.

**Sherbert –** A frozen fruit-flavored mixture similar to an ice, but with milk, egg white, or gelatin.

**Shish kebab –** A method of cooking developed by Nomadic sheep herdsmen in the Near East who found that they could roast lamb or mutton over their campfire by cutting the meat into small pieces and thrusting it onto a skewer and cooked over the fire. The Shish means a skewer and kebab means roast meat. In Russia its called Shashik and in France its called en brochette.

**Should –** Highly recommended, advisory procedure (FDA).

**Shortening –** A fat substance (lard, butter, hydrogenated oil) used in baked products to give a crisp and light texture.

**Shred –** To cut or tear into small, usually long, narrow pieces.

**Simmer** – To cook slowly in a liquid at a temperature of 185 degree F. or lower.

**Skewer** – A long pin of wood or metal on which food or meat is held while cooking.

**Smell** – To detect an odor or scent by the olfactory nerve.

**Smoked** – Products which have been dried or cured and wood smoke deposited on them.

**Smoke Point** – The temperature at which a fat or oil gives off a thin continuous stream of smoke. A sign of imminent breakdown of the fat or oil.

**Smorgasbord** – A table with a variety of food, chiefly cold cuts of fish or meat.

**Sodium Free** – Less than 5 mg of sodium per serving.

**Solid Pack** – Fruits packed without any added liquid or syrup.

**Soluble Fibers** – Pectins, gums, and certain hemicelluloses. They lower the absorption of cholesterol, regulate blood sugars, remove toxic chemicals and carcinogens from the body.

**Soluble Solids** – The solids in solution which are largely made up of sucrose and other sugars, fruit acids, and some mineral salts.

**Sorbet** – Fat free ices relatively low in calories and may be flavored with fruits, fruit juices, or pectins.

**Sorbitol** – A natural occurring sweet (about 40% as sweet as sucrose) substance found in many fruits, algae, and seaweed.

**Souffle** – A spongy hot dish made light in baking by stiffly beaten egg whites.

**Soup** – A liquid food made by boiling meat, vegetables, fish, etc. in water with various seasoning agents.

**Sour** – A taste sensation of which the taste is primarily acidic.

**Sourdough Bread** – Bread made with sourdough cultures instead of yeast.

**Spaghetti** – Pasta made of wheat, like macaroni, but is solid not tubular.

**Spatzle** – Dough forced through a coarse colander or sieve to form noodles, usually used with stews or goulash.

**Specification** – A specification is basically a communication tool to define reasonable expectations. A specification serves as the body of rules for the manufacture and sale of food products. A specification describes the product, process or material in specific terms. It should always be written and it should be objective.

**Specific Gravity** – A measure of the total solids content of a product; the ratio of the weight of a given sample in air to the same weight of that sample in water at 25 degree C.

**Spice** – Aromatic natural products which may be dried seeds, buds, fruits or flower parts, bark, or roots of plants usually of tropical origin.

**Spit** – Utensil in which meat, etc. can be roasted before a fire.

**Spoilage** – A product that has lost its valuable qualities, e.g., rotten, rancid, etc.

**Spore** – The resting stage in the growth cycle of certain bacteria (rod shaped) which are resistant to heat and chemicals. In the case of yeast and molds, spores are considered reproductive bodies since many spores are produced by one organism.

**Stabilizer** – A food additive that thickens, prevents separation, prevents flavor deterioration, retards oxidation by increasing the viscosity and gives a smoother consistency to the product, such as, agar and egg albumin.

**Stale** – A dried out food, one that is not fresh.

**Standard Deviation (Sigma)** – The square root of the mean square of the deviations from the mean-A statistic used to express the amount of variation in a set of data.

**Standard of Fill of Container (FDA)** – A statement which establishes the minimum weight or volume of a specific food which the container must hold, as determined by procedures specified in the standard, below which the food product is of substandard fill of container and must be clearly labeled "Below Standard of Fill".

**Standard of Quality (FDA)** – A statement which establishes a minimum quality for a specific food product below which it is of substandard quality and must be clearly labeled "Below Standard of Quality Good Food—Not High Grade".

**Standards of Identity (FDA)** – Regulations issued by the U.S. Food and Drug Administration to define the allowable ingredients, composition and other characteristics of food products.

**Standard Plate Count** – A method used to determine the number of specific microorganisms present in foods, other substances, or surfaces.

**Starch** – White, odorless, and tasteless carbohydrates produced by plants as an energy store.

**Staphyloccus** – Any of various spherical Gram-positive bacteria including some that cause acute intestinal disturbances and infections.

**Staple** – Food products essential for daily consumption.

**Starve** – To perish from hunger.

**Statistic** – An estimate of a parameter, based on a given sample. A sample average is a statistic as is a sample standard deviation or range.

**Steep** – To extract in liquid just below the boiling point of water.

**Steam** – To cook food, usually on a rack over simmering liquid with or without pressure.

**Stems and Shoots as foods** – Asparagus, Celery, Kohlrabi, and rhubarb.

**Sterile** – A product that contains no microorganisms.

**Sterilization** – The process of destruction of micro-organisms by heat or radiation.

**Stew** – A slowly cooked dish containing meat and/or vegetables with seasoning and a sauce.

**Stir** – To mix ingredients with a circular motion, that is to blend ingredients or food.

**Stock** – Culinary preparation, fat or lean, used to make sauces and broth for thickening, flavoring and glazing.

**Streptococcus** – A type of spherical bacteria.

**Stroganoff** – A beef dish sauteed with onions and prepared with a cream sauce, mushrooms, and gravy.

**Stuffing** – Dressing placed in meat, poultry or fish.

**Style** – The form in which a product is made, e.g., whole, half, etc.

**Subjective** – Pertaining to an individual experience which can be observed and reported only by the person involved.

**Sublimation** – The physical process by which a substance passes directly from the solid state to the vapor or gas state, such as the evaporation of ice during freeze-drying.

**Sucrose (Sugar)** – A 12 carbon disaccahride sugar found in sugar cane or sugar beets and made up of one molecule of fructose and glucose.

**Sucrose polyester** –   An artificial fat.

**Sugar** – Sweet carbohydrate obtained directly from the juices of plants or indirectly from the hydrolysis of starch.

**Sundae** – Composite sweet, usually made with ice cream and syrups.

**Surfactant** – Surface active agent capable of breaking the surface tension of particles.

**Sweet** – A quality of taste sensation of which the taste of sucrose is the typical example.

**Swell** – A can or jar or package of food in which gas production has caused expansion.

**Syneresis** – The contraction of a gel when left standing.

**Synthesize** – To build up a compound by the union of simpler compounds, that is, sucrose from two simpler sugars-glucose and fructose.

**Syrup** – Liquid made with sugar and water used as for the canning of fruit. The strength of the syrup is measured on a Brix or Baume scale and it is classified as Extra Heavy meaning 60 to 70% sugar, Heavy syrup containing 40 to 55% sugar, Medium syrup containing from 25 to 30% sugar, and Light syrup containing from 10 to 20% sugar. These levels of syrup concentration are called "Put-In" values and the level of syrup after it has equalized with the fruit following canning is called the "Cut-Out" value. An extra Heavy Put In Syrup will cut out between 22 and 35 degree Brix or percent sugar, while a Heavy syrup will cut out between 18 and 33 degree Brix or percent sugar, and a Light syrup will cut out between 14 to 18 degree Brix or percent sugar. The difference between the "Put-In" and the "Cut-Out" value is due to the maturity or the sugar content of the fruit at the time of packing. (See Appendix Table).

# T

**Table d'horte** — A complete restaurant meal at a fixed price.

**Taffy** – A confection made from brown sugar or molasses and repeatedly stretched or pulled until porous and light-colored.

**Tannins** – A stringent bitter phenolic compound.

**Tare** – Generally means the weight of the empty container or package.

**Tart** – Sharp or pungent taste.

**Taste** – To eat, drink, or bite a product; to distinguish the four gustatory qualities of food, e.g., sweet, salt, sour, or bitter.

**Taste Bud** – Receptors found in the mouth.

**Taste Panel** – A selected group of people (Observers, Judges) who perform organoleptic evaluations of food products.

**Tempeh** – A fermented (*Rhizopus odigosperm* – a mold) soybean product.

**Tempura** – A method of cooking raw fish, meat, or vegetables by coating them in a thin cold batter and quickly deep frying them in hot oil.

**Texture** – Properties of food that deal with roughness, smoothness, graininess, etc.

**Thermal Death Time** – Time required to inactivate a specific microbial population in a food at any given temperature–based on the F value.

**Thermal Process** – The application of heat to food, either before or after sealing the food in a hermetically sealed container, for a period of time and at a temperature scientifically determined to achieve a condition of commercial sterility (i.e.,

**Thermal Process** — Continued
the destruction of microorganisms of public health significance as well as those capable of reproducing in the food under normal non-refrigerated conditions).

**Thermoduric** – Microorganisms that have the ability to withstand high temperatures, that is, are highly heat resistant.

**Thermophiles** – Bacteria which grow optimally above 113 degree F.

**Thermophillic Bacteria** – Bacteria which grow in a range from 40 to 90 degree C. with an optimum growth range from 55 to 65 degree C.

**Thicken** – To make a thin, smooth paste by mixing together Arrowroot, cornstarch, or flour with an equal amount of cold water by stirring into hot liquid and continued stirring until thick.

**Thickening Agent** – A texturizer, such as starch and gelatin, which increases the consistency of a product.

**Threshold** – The level below which there is no response to a stimulus.

**Titration** – A method of determining the strength of a solution in terms of the smallest amount of the solution required to produce a given effect in reaction with another solution or substance.

**Toast** – To brown or warm or cook by dry heat.

**Tocopherol** – An antioxidant found naturally in vegetable oil that retards the onset of rancidity.

**Toffee** – A candy made of butter, sugar, and milk but cooked at a higher temperature than caramels.

**Tofu** – A fermented soybean product resembling cottage cheese.

**Torte** – A round cake made with eggs and sugar and sometimes covered with frosting.

**Tortilla** – A circular unleavened flat bread made out of coarse corn meal water and lime that is partially dried and kept refrigerated until used.

**Tortilla Chip** – A corn meal product that is fryed and dryed and which may be seasoned.

**Toss** – To tumble ingredients lightly with a lifting motion.

**Tournedos** – Small slices taken from the heart of the fillet of beef thin cut and sauteed or grilled and garnished prior to serving.

**Toxin** – A poisonous product produced by micro-organisms.

**Toxicology** – The science of poisons and their antidotes.

**Translucent** – Capable of transmitting some light, but not clear enough to see through.

**Transparent** – Material capable of a high degree of light transmission.

**Triangle Testing** – A method of difference testing in which three coded samples are presented to the judge or observer or panelist and they are asked to identify the different or odd sample.

**Tristimulus** – A colorimetric specification of color based on three measurements for hue, value and chroma.

**Triticale** – A high protein cereal grain.

**Troy** – A system of weights based on a pound equals 12 ounces.

**Truffle** – Edible fungi which grows underground, very delicate– French truffles are black while italian truffles are white.

**Trypsin** – An enzyme from the pancreas used to tenderize meats.

**Tubers** – Jerusalem Artichoke and White or Irish potatoes.

**Type** – A specific variety of food, such as Freestone peaches vs. Clingstone peaches.

**Ultraviolet** – Wavelength of radiation that is shorter than visible light and often used for sterilization of some products.

**Unsalted** – Foods that carry only the sodium naturally present in the ingredients.

**Unsaturated** – A term descriptive of the carbon-hydrogen make-up of the fatty acid portion of a fat or oil. The term refers specifically to a shortage of hydrogen atoms in the oil's molecular structure. The less the hydrogen content, the greater the degree of unsaturation and the greater the reactivity with oxygen. Highly unsaturated oils tend to become rancid quicker than less unsaturated oils unless they contain antioxidants.

**Upper Control Limit for the Average** – A system of determining the pattern that sample averages should follow if a constant system of choice is operating.

# V

**Vacuum** – A space empty of air.

**Variable** – Procedures based on actual values in terms of numerical scales in contrast to attributes where each item is designated merely as acceptable or unacceptable.

**Variance** – A measure of variation equal to the square of the standard deviation or its estimate.

**Vegetarian** – A person that does not consume meats, poultry or fish, but may eat butter, milk and eggs.

**Vegetative Cells** – Stage of active growth of micro-organisms, as opposed to bacterial spore.

**Veloute Sauce** – Thickened butter and flour with fish stock.

**Vermicelli** – A pasta whose descriptive name suggests its wormlike form-used in soups, souffles, salads, etc.

**Vichysoise** – Potatoes liquidifed, cooked, chilled, and served cold with a sprinkling of chives.

**Vignette** – A small decorative design on the label.

**Vinaigrette** – A mixture of oil and vinegar seasoned with salt and pepper and sometimes the addition of herbs.

**Vintage** – Fruit or wine of any given season.

**Viscosity** – The numerical index of the resistance to flow of a Newtonian fluid.

**Vitamin** – A group of essential micronutrients for man.

**Vitamin A** – Fat Soluble vitamin, unsaponifiable, heat and oxygen labile liquid. Occurs in body as a fatty acid ester. Found in yellow pigments of most vegetables and fruits. Essential for integrity of epithelial cells, a stimulus for new cell growth, aids in maintaining resistance to infections, increases longevity and delays senility.

**Vitamin B₁ (Thiamin)** – Water soluble vitamin, comparatively stable toward dry heat but destroyed by high heat and sulfites. Essential for maintenance of good appetite, normal digestion and gastrointestinal tonus. It is necessary for growth, fertility and lactation, it is needed for normal functioning of nervous tissue and cardiac musculature. It is not stored in the body and must be replenished almost daily.

**Vitamin B₂ (Riboflavin)** – Slightly soluble in water, very bitter taste, and very soluble in alkali. Essential for many enzymatic reactions in the body and control of certain body functions. Symptoms of deficiency are corneal vascularization, cloudiness, ulceration, cataracts, hotolphobia, dimness of vision, burning and itching of the eyes, impairment of visual acuity, congestion of the sclera, and abnormal pigmentation of the iris. The skin may show atrophy of the epidermis.

**Vitamin B₆ (Pyridoxine)** – Soluble in water, stable to heat, but not light. Functions as a co-enzyme. Essential for complete metabolism of tryptophan and fats and fatty acids. Excellent sources are Wheat bran, wheat germ, wheat flour, brewers and bakers yeast, soybeans, molasses, liver and yellow corn.

**Biotin** – Soluble in water, heat stable, light insensitive. Exists in yeast and animal products in a combined water-insoluble form, whereas that occuring in vegetables and plants is water-soluble. Functions as a co-enzyme. Good sources are peanuts, peas, liver, filberts, mushrooms, eggs, chocolate and cauliflower.

**Vitamin B₁₂** – Water soluble, heat stable in neutral solutions. Essential for normal development of red blood cells and treatment of pernicious anemia. Found in liver and kidney and muscle meats.

**Vitamin C –** (Asorbic Acid) – Freely soluble in water, very unstable and most sensitive to alkalies and oxidation especially in presence of iron and copper. Essential for the formation of intercellular substances, tooth formation, bone formation and repair, and wound healing. Scurvy is a classical manifestation of severe deficiency. Found widely in most fruits and many vegetables.

**Vitamin D –** Soluble in fat, stable to heat and oxidation and is formed from irradiation of sterols. Essential for enhancement of calcium and phosphorous from the intestinal tract, prevents rickets (cheifly affecting bones and teeth). Found in cod liver oil, halibut fish, sardines, mackerel, and other canned fish.

**Vitamin E - (Tocopherols) –** Fat soluble vitamin. Functions in promoting reproduction and intracellular antioxidant. Found in Wheat germ oil, seeds, spinach, lettuce, egg yolk, vegetable oils, meat and milk.

**Vitamin K –** Mostly fat soluble and heat stable. Essential for normal blood clotting. Found in alfalfa, cabbage, cauliflower, spinach, soybeans and pork liver.

**Folic Acid –** Soluble in water. Necessary for the production of red and white blood cells. Food sources include Liver, kidney, dried beans, beef, yeast, green leafy vegetables, wheat, and mushrooms.

**Niacin- (Nicotinic Acid) –** Soluble in hot water, stable to air, light, heat, acids and alkalies. Functions as a co-enzyme. Deficiency is human pellagra, skin erruption, loss of appetitie, nausea, vomiting and abdominal pain, dialation of blood vessels and atrophy, lesions in the colon, diarrhea, and disruption of the nervous system. Food sources are liver, kidney, meat, yeasts, cereals, legumes, green and leafy vegetables.

**Vitamins –** Continued

   **Pantothenic Acid –** Acid-Soluble in water, stable to oxidizing and reducing agents, and labile to dry heat, hot alkali or hot acid. Essential for all living organisms including man, to maintain normal skin, normal growth, and normal development of the central nervous system. Food sources are yeast, meats, egg yolks, dairy products, and green leafy vegetables.

# W

**Wafer** – A thin cake or cracker.

**Waffle** – A cake made from pancake batter and cooked in a mold.

**Water Activity ($A_w$)** – A measure of the free moisture in a product. It is determined by dividing water vapor pressure of the substance by the vapor pressure of pure water at the same temperature.

**Water Hardness** – The amount of minerals in the water, e.g., Soft water has 0-60 ppm, Moderately Hard water has 60-120 ppm, Hard water has 120-180 ppm, and Very Hard water has over 180 ppm of Calcium, Magnesium or other minerals.

**Water pack** – Fruit packed in water without the addition of any sugar or syrup.

**Wavelength** – A unit used to measure light waves— Angstrom.

**Wetting Agents** – A surface active agent used to break or lower the surface tension of water.

**Watt** – A measure of power or rate of energy.

**Whey** – The liquid and its dissolved lactose, minerals, and other minor constituents remaining after milk has been coagulated to separate the curd. Curd is made up of caesin, most of the fat, and some lactose, water and the minerals from milk.

**Whip** – To beat rapidly to incorporate air and produce expansion.

**Wok** – A bowl shaped cooking vessel used especially in the preparation of Chinese foods.

**Wort** – The liquid fraction separated from the mash by filtration after the digestion of the mash is completed.

# XYZ

**Yeast** – A microscopic plant that can convert sugar to carbon dioxide. It is used as a leavening agent in foods and as a fermentation agent in alcoholic fermentation.

**Yogurt** – A custard like product made by fermenting concentrated whole or skimmed milk with or without added fruits or flavorings.

**Z value** – Number of degrees F. required for a specific thermal death curve to pass through one Log cycle.

**Zwieback** – A loaf that is baked, sliced, and toasted.

# Glossary Appedix
# Charts and Tables Index

## TABLE 1

### BOILING POINT OF WATER
### AT VARIOUS ALTITUDES

| Altitude | Boiling Point degree F. |
|----------|-------------------------|
| 0 | 212.0 |
| 500 | 211.2 |
| 1000 | 210.2 |
| 1500 | 209.2 |
| 2000 | 208.3 |
| 2500 | 207.4 |
| 3000 | 206.4 |
| 3500 | 205.5 |
| 4000 | 204.4 |
| 4500 | 203.6 |
| 5000 | 202.6 |
| 5500 | 201.7 |
| 6000 | 200.7 |

**TABLE 2**

**Comparison Table "Avoirdupois to Metric"**

| Pounds-Grams | | Ounces-Grams | | Ounces-Grams | |
|---|---|---|---|---|---|
| 1 | 453.6 | 1 | 28.4 | 1/16 | 1.77 |
| 2 | 907.2 | 2 | 56.7 | 1/8 | 3.54 |
| 3 | 1360.8 | 3 | 85.1 | 3/16 | 5.32 |
| 4 | 1814.4 | 4 | 113.4 | 1/4 | 7.09 |
| 5 | 2268.0 | 5 | 141.8 | 5/16 | 8.56 |
| 6 | 2721.5 | 6 | 170.1 | 3/8 | 10.6 |
| 7 | 3175.1 | 7 | 198.4 | 7/16 | 12.4 |
| 8 | 3628.7 | 8 | 226.8 | 1/2 | 14.2 |
| 9 | 4082.3 | 9 | 255.2 | 9/16 | 16.0 |
| 10 | 4535.9 | 10 | 283.5 | 5/8 | 17.7 |
| 11 | 4989.5 | 11 | 311.9 | 11/16 | 19.5 |
| 12 | 5443.1 | 12 | 340.2 | 3/4 | 21.3 |
| | | 13 | 368.6 | 13/16 | 23.0 |
| | | 14 | 396.9 | 7/8 | 24.8 |
| | | 15 | 425.3 | 15/16 | 26.6 |
| | | 16 | 453.6 | 1 | 28.4 |

## TABLE 3

### Comparison Table for Liquid Measure

1 fl oz =   29.6 ml
2 fl oz =   59.2 ml
3 fl oz =   88.7 ml
4 fl oz = 118.3 ml
5 fl oz = 147.8 ml
6 fl oz = 177.4 ml
7 fl oz = 207.0 ml
8 fl oz = 236.6 ml
9 fl oz = 266.2 ml

1 qt = 0.946L
2 qt = 1.89L
3 qt = 2.84L
4 qt = 3.79L

1 ml = 0.034 fl oz.
2 ml = 0.07   fl oz.
3 ml = 0.10   fl oz.
4 ml = 0.14   fl oz.
5 ml = 0.17   fl oz.
6 ml = 0.20   fl oz.
7 ml = 0.24   fl oz.
8 ml = 0.27   fl oz.
9 ml = 0.30   fl oz.

**TABLE 4**

| Conversion Table<br>"Fractions to Decimals" | |
|---|---|
| 1/64 = .015625 | 33/64 = .515625 |
| 1/32 = .03125 | 17/32 = .53125 |
| 3/64 = .046875 | 35/64 = .546875 |
| 1/16 = .0625 | 9/16 = .5625 |
| 5/64 = .078125 | 37/64 = .578125 |
| 3/32 = .09375 | 19/32 = .59375 |
| 7/64 = .109375 | 39/64 = .609375 |
| 1/8 = .125 | 5/8 = .625 |
| 9/64 = .140625 | 41/64 = .640625 |
| 5/32 = .15625 | 21/32 = .65625 |
| 11/64 = .171875 | 43/64 = .671875 |
| 3/16 = .1875 | 11/16 = .6875 |
| 13/64 = .203125 | 45/64 = .703125 |
| 7/32 = .21875 | 23/32 = .71875 |
| 15/64 = .234375 | 47/64 = .734375 |
| 1/4 = .25 | 3/4 = .75 |
| 17/64 = .265625 | 49/64 = .765625 |
| 9/32 = .28125 | 25/32 = .78125 |
| 19/64 = .296875 | 51/64 = .796875 |
| 5/16 = .3125 | 13/16 = .8125 |
| 21/64 = .328125 | 53/64 = .828125 |
| 11/32 = .34375 | 27/32 = .84375 |
| 23/64 = .359375 | 55/64 = .859375 |
| 3/8 = .375 | 7/8 = .875 |
| 25/64 = .390625 | 57/64 = .890625 |
| 13/32 = .40625 | 29/32 = .90625 |
| 27/64 = .421875 | 59/64 = .921875 |
| 7/16 = .4375 | 15/16 = .9375 |
| 29/64 = .453125 | 61/64 = .953125 |
| 15/32 = .46875 | 31/32 = .96875 |
| 31/64 = .484375 | 63/64 = .984375 |
| 1/2 = .5 | 1 = 1 |

## TABLE 5

### Conversion Inches to Millimeters

| Inches | Millimeters(mm.) |
|---|---|
| 1/8 equals | 3.2 |
| 1/4 equals | 6.4 |
| 3/8 equals | 9.5 |
| 1/2 equals | 12.7 |
| 5/8 equals | 15.9 |
| 3/4 equals | 19.1 |
| 7/8 equals | 22.2 |
| 1 equals | 25.4 |
| 1 1/2 equals | 38.1 |
| 2 equals | 50.8 |
| 2 1/2 equals | 63.5 |

## TABLE 6

### English And Metric Equivalents

| | | |
|---|---|---|
| 1 grain | = | 64.79 mg |
| 1 dram | = | 1.77 g |
| 1 gram | = | 0.035 oz |
| 1 oz | = | 28.35 g |
| 1 Kg | = | 2.205 lb |
| 1 lb | = | 453.5 g |
| | | |
| 1 fl oz | = | 29.47L |
| 1 ml | = | 0.0334 fl oz |
| 1 Tsp | = | 4.93 ml (60 drops) |
| 1 Tbsp | = | 14.79 ml |
| 1 Cup | = | 236.6 ml (8 oz) |
| 1 L | = | 1.057 Qt |
| 1 Qt | = | 0.946 L (1 gal) (128 oz) |
| 1 Gal | = | 3.785 L |
| | | |
| 1 In | = | 2.54 cm |
| 1 ft | = | 30.45 cm |
| 1 yd | = | 91.44 M |
| 1 cm | = | .3937 in |
| 1 M | = | 1.0936 yd |

## TABLE 7

| Moisture Content in Fresh Fruits & Vegetables | | | |
|---|---|---|---|
| Product | Average | Maximum | Minimum |
| Apples | 84.1 | 90.9 | 78.7 |
| Apricots | 85.4 | 91.5 | 81.9 |
| Avocados | 65.4 | 68.4 | 60.9 |
| Blackberries | 85.3 | 89.4 | 78.4 |
| Cherries, sweet | 80.0 | 83.9 | 74.7 |
| Figs | 78.0 | 88.0 | 50.0 |
| Grapefruit | 88.0 | 93.1 | 86.0 |
| Grapes–European | 81.6 | 87.1 | 74.8 |
| Muskmelon | 92.8 | 96.5 | 87.5 |
| Oranges | 87.2 | 89.9 | 83.0 |
| Peaches | 86.9 | 90.0 | 81.9 |
| Pears | 82.7 | 86.1 | 75.9 |
| Prunes (fresh) | 76.5 | 89.3 | 61.6 |
| Rhubarb | 94.9 | 96.8 | 92.6 |
| Watermelons | 92.1 | 92.9 | 91.3 |
| Artichokes | 83.7 | 85.8 | 81.6 |
| Asparagus | 93.0 | 94.4 | 90.8 |
| Snap Beans | 88.9 | 94.0 | 78.8 |
| Lima Beans | 66.5 | 71.8 | 58.9 |
| Beets | 87.6 | 94.1 | 82.3 |
| Cabbage | 92.4 | 94.8 | 88.4 |
| Carrots | 88.2 | 91.1 | 83.1 |
| Cauliflower | 91.7 | 93.8 | 87.6 |
| Celery, stalks | 93.7 | 95.2 | 89.9 |
| Corn, sweet | 73.9 | 86.1 | 61.3 |
| Cucumber | 96.1 | 97.3 | 94.7 |
| Lettuce | 94.8 | 97.4 | 91.5 |
| Onions | 89.2 | 92.6 | 80.3 |
| Peas, green | 74.3 | 84.1 | 56.7 |
| Potatoes | 77.8 | 85.2 | 66.0 |
| Pumpkin | 90.5 | 94.6 | 84.4 |
| Spinach | 92.7 | 95.0 | 89.4 |
| Tomatoes | 94.1 | 96.7 | 90.6 |

Source: Part from Joslyn (1950).

**TABLE 8**

| Nutritional Requirements | | |
|---|---|---|
| Nutrient and Unit of Measurememt | U.S. RDA[1] | Amount Per 100 Kilocalories |
| Protein (optional), gram (g) | [2]65 | 3.25 |
|  | 45 | 2.25 |
| Vitamin A, international unit (UI) | 5000 | 250 |
| Vitamin C, milligram (mg) | 60 | 3 |
| Thiamine, milligram (mg) | 1.5 | 0.075 |
| Riboflavin, milligram (mg) | 1.7 | 0.085 |
| Niacin, milligram (mg) | 20 | 1.0 |
| Calcium, gram (g) | 1 | 0.05 |
| Iron, milligram (mg) | 18 | 0.9 |
| Vitamin D (optional), international unit (IU) | 400 | 20 |
| Vitamin E, international unit (IU) | 30 | 1.5 |
| Vitamin B-6, milligram (mg) | 2 | 0.1 |
| Folic acid, milligram (mg) | 0.4 | 0.02 |
| Vitamin B-12, microgram (mcg) | 6 | 0.3 |
| Phosphoprus, gram (g) | 1 | 0.05 |
| Iodine (optional), microgram (mcg) | 150 | 7.5 |
| Magnesium, milligram (mg) | 400 | 20 |
| Zinc, milligram (mg) | 15 | 0.75 |
| Copper, milligram (mg) | 2 | 0.1 |
| Biotin, milligram (mg) | 0.3 | 0.015 |
| Pantothenic acid, milligram (mg) | 10 | 0.5 |
| Potassium, gram (g) | [3] | 0.125 |
| Manganese, milligram (mg) | [3] | 0.2 |

[1] U.S. Recommended Daily Allowance (U.S. RDA) for adults and children 4 or more years of age.

[2] If the protein efficiency ratio is equal to or better than that of casein, the U.S. RDA is 45 g.

[3] No U.S. RDA has been established for either potassium or manganese; daily dietary intakes of 2.5 g. and 4.0 mg., respectively, are based on the 1979 Recommended Dietary Allowances of the Food and Nutrition Board, National Academy of Sciences – National Research Council.

**TABLE 9**

## Per Capita Consumption
## Selected Foods — Average During
## Past 20 Years With Trends Indicated

| FOOD ITEM | POUNDS | TRENDS* |
|---|---|---|
| Total Red Meat (Excluding game) | 143.7 | > |
| Beef | 75.5 | > |
| Pork | 63.8 | > |
| Lamb and Mutton | 2.7 | < |
| Veal | 3.0 | < |
| Fishery Products | 11.8 | > |
| Chicken | 39.8 | >> |
| Turkey | 8.3 | > |
| Eggs | 39.1 | < |
| Fluid Whole Milk | 163.9 | << |
| Total Cheese | 12.6 | >> |
| Butter | 5.8 | < |
| Ice Cream | 17.9 | — |
| Fat & Oils · Total Fat Food Content | 52.1 | > |
| Total Fruit | 139.6 | > |
| Processed | 54.5 | > |
| Fresh | 85.1 | — |
| Total Vegetables | 154.2 | > |
| Fresh (Commercial) | 97.7 | > |
| Processed | 56.5 | — |
| Wheat Flour | 116.0 | > |
| Sugar | 94.9 | < |
| Corn Sweetners | 26.0 | >>> |
| Coffee | 7.6 | < |
| Soft Drinks | 25.0 | >>> |
| TOTAL | 1497.2 | |

* > = increasing, < = decreasing, — = No significant trend

**TABLE 10**

## pH VALUES OF SOME COMMERCIALLY CANNED FOODS

| Canned Product | pH Values | | |
|---|---|---|---|
| | Avg. | Min. | Max. |
| Apples | 3.4 | 3.2 | 3.7 |
| Apple Cider | 3.3 | 3.3 | 3.5 |
| Applesauce | 3.6 | 3.2 | 4.2 |
| Apricots | 3.7 | 3.6 | 3.9 |
| Apricots, strained | 4.1 | 3.8 | 4.3 |
| Asparagus, green | 5.5 | 5.4 | 5.6 |
| Asparagus, white | 5.5 | 5.4 | 5.7 |
| Asparagus, pureed | 5.2 | 5.0 | 5.3 |
| Beans, baked | 5.9 | 5.6 | 5.9 |
| Beans, green | 5.4 | 5.2 | 5.7 |
| Beans, green, pureed | 5.1 | 5.0 | 5.2 |
| Beans, lima | 6.2 | 6.0 | 6.3 |
| Beans, lima, pureed | 5.8 | — | — |
| Beans, red kidney | 5.9 | 5.7 | 6.1 |
| Beans, and Pork | 5.6 | 5.0 | 6.0 |
| Beans, wax | 5.3 | 5.2 | 5.5 |
| Beans, wax, pureed | 5.0 | 4.9 | 5.1 |
| Beets | 5.4 | 5.0 | 5.8 |
| Beets, Pureed | 5.3 | 5.0 | 5.5 |
| Blackberries | 3.6 | 3.2 | 4.1 |
| Blueberries | 3.4 | 3.3 | 3.5 |
| Carrots | 5.2 | 5.0 | 5.4 |
| Carrots, pureed | 5.1 | 4.9 | 5.2 |
| Cherries, black | 4.0 | 3.9 | 4.1 |
| Cherries, red sour | 3.3 | 3.3 | 3.5 |
| Cherries, Royal Ann | 3.9 | 3.8 | 3.9 |
| Cherry juice | 3.4 | 3.4 | 3.4 |
| Corn, W.K., brine packed | 6.3 | 6.1 | 6.8 |
| Corn, cream style | 6.1 | 5.9 | 6.3 |
| Corn, on cob | 6.1 | 6.1 | 6.1 |
| Cranberry juice | 2.6 | 2.6 | 2.7 |
| Cranberry sauce | 2.6 | 2.4 | 2.8 |
| Figs | 5.0 | 5.0 | 5.0 |
| Gooseberries | 2.9 | 2.8 | 3.2 |
| Grapes, purple | 3.1 | 3.1 | 3.1 |
| Grape juice | 3.2 | 2.9 | 3.7 |
| Grapefruit | 3.2 | 3.0 | 3.4 |

Continued next page

## TABLE 10 —Continued

### pH VALUES OF SOME COMMERCIALLY CANNED FOODS (Continued)

| Canned Product | pH Values | | |
| --- | --- | --- | --- |
| | Avg. | Min. | Max. |
| Grapefruit juice | 3.3 | 3.0 | 3.4 |
| Lemon juice | 2.4 | 2.3 | 2.6 |
| Loganberries | 2.9 | 2.7 | 3.3 |
| Mushrooms | 5.8 | 5.8 | 5.9 |
| Olives, green | 3.4 | — | — |
| Olives, ripe | 6.9 | 5.9 | 7.3 |
| Orange juice | 3.7 | 3.5 | 4.0 |
| Peaches | 3.8 | 3.6 | 4.1 |
| Pears, Bartlett | 4.1 | 3.6 | 4.7 |
| Peas. Alaska, (Wisc) | 6.2 | 6.0 | 6.3 |
| Peas, sweet wrinkled | 6.2 | 5.9 | 6.5 |
| Peas, pureed | 5.9 | 5.8 | 6.0 |
| Pickles, dill | 3.1 | 2.6 | 3.8 |
| Pickles, fresh cucumber | 4.4 | 4.4 | 4.4 |
| Pickles, sour | 3.1 | 3.1 | 3.1 |
| Pickles, sweet | 2.7 | 2.5 | 3.0 |
| Pineapple, crushed | 3.4 | 3.2 | 3.5 |
| Pineapple, sliced | 3.5 | 3.5 | 3.6 |
| Pineapple tidbits | 3.5 | 3.4 | 3.7 |
| Pineapple juice | 3.5 | 3.4 | 3.5 |
| Plums, green gage | 3.8 | 3.6 | 4.0 |
| Plums Victoria | 3.0 | 2.8 | 3.1 |
| Potatoes, sweet | 5.2 | 5.1 | 5.4 |
| Potatoes, white | 5.5 | 5.4 | 5.6 |
| Prunes, fr. prune plums | 3.7 | 2.5 | 4.2 |
| Pumpkin | 5.1 | 4.8 | 5.2 |
| Raspberries, black | 3.7 | 3.2 | 4.1 |
| Raspberries, red | 3.1 | 2.8 | 3.5 |
| Sauerkraut | 3.5 | 3.4 | 3.7 |
| Spaghetti in tomato sauce | 5.1 | 4.7 | 5.5 |
| Spinach | 5.4 | 5.1 | 5.9 |
| Spinach, pureed | 5.4 | 5.2 | 5.5 |
| Strawberries | 3.4 | 3.0 | 3.9 |
| Tomatoes | 4.4 | 4.0 | 4.6 |
| Tomato juice | 4.3 | 4.0 | 4.5 |
| Tomato, pureed | 4.2 | 4.0 | 4.3 |

## TABLE 11

### RELATIONSHIP OF PUT-IN (P-I) SYRUP VERSUS CUT-OUT (C-O) SYRUP BY LABEL REQUIREMENTS FOR STANDARDIZED FRUIT PRODUCTS

(All Data in % of Brix Values)

| Product | Extra Heavy P-I | Extra Heavy C-O | Heavy P-I | Heavy C-O | Light P-I | Light C-O | Slightly Sweetned P-I | Slightly Sweetned C-O |
|---|---|---|---|---|---|---|---|---|
| Apricots | 55 or more | 25–40 | 35–55 | 21–25 | 15–30 | 16–21 | 10–15 | less than 16 |
| Berries | | | | | | | | |
| Black | 40 or more | 24–35 | 30–40 | 19–24 | 20–30 | 14–19 | 10–20 | less than 14 |
| Blue | 40 or more | 25–35 | 30–40 | 20–25 | 20–30 | 15–20 | 10–20 | less than 15 |
| Boysen | 40 or more | 24–35 | 30–40 | 19–24 | 20–30 | 14–19 | 10–20 | less than14 |
| Dew | 40 or more | 24–35 | 30–40 | 19–24 | 20–30 | 14–19 | 10–20 | less than 14 |
| Goose | 40 or more | 26–35 | 30–40 | 20–26 | 20–30 | 14–20 | 10–20 | less than 14 |
| Huckle | 40 or more | 25–35 | 30–40 | 20–25 | 20–30 | 15–20 | 10–20 | less than 15 |
| Logan | 40 or more | 24–35 | 30–40 | 19–24 | 20–30 | 14–19 | 10–20 | less than 14 |
| Black Rasp. | 40 or more | 27–35 | 30–40 | 20–27 | 20–30 | 14–20 | 10–20 | less than 14 |
| Red Rasp. | 40 or more | 28–35 | 30–40 | 22–28 | 20–30 | 14–22 | 10–20 | less than 14 |
| Straw. | 40 or more | 27–35 | 30–40 | 19–27 | 20–30 | 14–19 | 10–20 | less than 14 |
| Young | 40 or more | 24–35 | 30–40 | 19–24 | 20–30 | 14–19 | 10–20 | less than 14 |
| RSP Cherries | 57 or more | 28–45 | 34–56 | 22–28 | 25–33 | 18–22 | 10–25 | less than 18 |
| Sweet Cherries | 45 or more | 25–35 | 30–45 | 20–25 | 15–25 | 16–20 | 10–15 | less than 16 |
| Figs | 40 or more | 26–35 | 30–40 | 21–26 | 20–30 | 16–21 | | |
| Fruit Cocktail | 40 or more | 22–35 | 36–38 | 18–22 | 30–34 | 14–18 | | |
| Peaches | 55 or more | 24–35 | 40–55 | 19–24 | 15–25 | 14–19 | 10–15 | less than 14 |
| Pears | 40 or more | 22–35 | 25–40 | 18–22 | 15–25 | 14–18 | 10–15 | less than 14 |
| Pineapple | 40 or more | 22–35 | 30–40 | 18–22 | 20–30 | 14–18 | | |
| Plums | | | | | | | | |
| Purple | 40 or more | 26–35 | 30–40 | 21–26 | 20–30 | 18–21 | 10–20 | less than 18 |
| Others | 40 or more | 24–35 | 30–40 | 19–24 | 20–30 | 16–19 | 10–20 | less than 16 |
| Prunes | 50 or more | 30–45 | 40–50 | 24–30 | 30–40 | 20–24 | | |
| Grapes | | | | | | | | |
| Seedless | 40 or more | 22–35 | 30–40 | 18–22 | 20–30 | 14–18 | 10–20 | less than 14 |

Put-In concentration must be varied depending on variety, muturity or area of production to obtain desired Cut-Out syrup concentration.

## TABLE 12

### Specific Heat of Foods
### B.T.U. Per lb. Per Degree F.

| | |
|---|---|
| Apples | 0.93 |
| Green Beans | 0.87 |
| Lima Beans | 0.75 |
| Beef | 0.69 |
| Berries | 0.93 |
| Bread | 0.68 |
| Butter | 0.50 |
| Carrots | 0.93 |
| Cream | 0.75 |
| Cucumbers | 0.98 |
| Fish (Fresh) | 0.86 |
| Fruits | 0.85 |
| Grains | 0.46 |
| Lamb | 0.93 |
| Onions | 0.91 |
| Pork | 0.82 |
| Potatoes | 0.86 |
| Spinach | 0.96 |

**TABLE 13**

## Approximate Shelf Life of Canned Fruits

| | |
|---|---|
| Apples | 30 Mo. |
| Apple Juice | 24 Mo. |
| Applesauce | 30 Mo. |
| Apricots | 24 Mo. |
| Berries | 18 Mo. |
| Cherries, RSP | 18 Mo. |
| Cherries, Sweet | 24 Mo. |
| Cranberry Sauce | 18 Mo. |
| Figs | 24 Mo. |
| Fruit Cocktail | 24 Mo. |
| Grapefruit Sections | 18 Mo. |
| Grape Juice | 14 Mo. |
| Orange Juice | 27 Mo. |
| Peaches | 27 Mo. |
| Pears | 28 Mo. |
| Pineapple | 24 Mo. |
| Pineapple Juice | 24 Mo. |
| Plums | 24 Mo. |

**TABLE 14**

## Approximate Shelf Life of Canned Vegetables

| | |
|---|---|
| Asparagus | 24 Mo. |
| Green Beans | 24 Mo. |
| Lima Beans | 36 Mo. |
| Beets | 18 Mo. |
| Carrots | 30 Mo. |
| Catsup (Glass) | 24 Mo. |
| Catsup (Metal) | 15 Mo. |
| Catsup (Plastic) | 18 Mo. |
| Chili Sauce (Glass) | 24 Mo. |
| Corn (WK) | 30 Mo. |
| Corn (CS) | 24 Mo. |
| Mushrooms | 20 Mo. |
| Okra | 18 Mo. |
| Peas | 20 Mo. |
| Pimentoes | 24 Mo. |
| Potatoes (Sweet) | 24 Mo. |
| Potatoes (Irish) | 20 Mo. |
| Pumpkin | 24 Mo. |
| Sauerkraut | 14 Mo. |
| Spinach | 24 Mo. |
| Tomatoes | 24 Mo. |
| Tomato Juice | 18 Mo. |
| Tomato Paste | 18 Mo. |

## TABLE 15

| Approximate Storage Life Of Frozen Foods At O Degree F. | |
|---|---|
| Beef | 10 Mo. |
| Breads (Quick) Baked | 2 Mo. |
| Breads (Yeast) Baked | 6 Mo. |
| Cakes | 6 Mo. |
| Candies | 1 Yr. |
| Cheese (Hard) | 1 Yr. |
| Cheese (Soft) | 4 Mo. |
| Cookies (Baked) | 6 Mo. |
| Eggs | 8 Mo. |
| Fish (Fatty) | 8 Mo. |
| Fish (Lean) | 1 Yr. |
| Fruits (No sugar) | 1 Yr. |
| Fruits (Unsugared) | 1½ Yr. |
| Ice Cream & Sherbets | 1½ Yr. |
| Lamb | 1 Yr. |
| Milk | 10 Mo. |
| Pastry (Unbaked) | 2 Mo. |
| Pork | 6 Mo. |
| Poultry | 6 Mo. |
| Sausage | 6 Mo. |
| Shellfish | 1 Yr. |
| Soups and Stews | 6 Mo. |
| Vegetables (Blanched) | 1 Yr. |

## TABLE 16

| TYLER STANDARD SCREEN SCALE SIEVES' | | | | | |
|---|---|---|---|---|---|
| Tyler Standard Screen Scale 2½ Opening in Inches | For Closer Sizing Ratio 2¼ Opening in Inches | Mesh | Diameter of Wire, Decimal of an Inch | U.S. Series Equivalents (Fine Series) | |
| | | | | Micron Designation | Number |
| 3 | — | — | 0.207 | — | — |
| 2 | — | — | 0.192 | — | — |
| 1.5 | — | — | 0.162 | — | — |
| 1.050 | 1.050 | — | 0.148 | — | — |
| — | 0.883 | — | 0.135 | — | — |
| 0.742 | 0.742 | — | 0.135 | — | — |
| — | 0.624 | — | 0.120 | — | — |
| 0.525 | 0.525 | — | 0.105 | — | — |
| — | 0.441 | — | 0.105 | — | — |
| 0.371 | 0.371 | — | 0.092 | — | — |
| — | 0.312 | 2½ | 0.088 | — | — |
| 0.263 | 0.263 | 3 | 0.070 | — | — |
| — | 0.221 | 3½ | 0.065 | 5660 | 3½ |
| 0.185 | 0.185 | 4 | 0.065 | 4760 | 4 |
| — | 0.156 | 5 | 0.044 | 4000 | 5 |
| 0.131 | 0.131 | 6 | 0.036 | 3360 | 6 |
| — | 0.110 | 7 | 0.0328 | 2830 | 7 |
| 0.093 | 0.093 | 8 | 0.032 | 2380 | 8 |
| — | 0.078 | 9 | 0.033 | 2000 | 10 |
| 0.065 | 0.065 | 10 | 0.035 | 1680 | 12 |
| — | 0.055 | 12 | 0.028 | 1410 | 14 |
| 0.046 | 0.046 | 14 | 0.025 | 1190 | 16 |
| — | 0.0390 | 16 | 0.0235 | 1000 | 18 |
| 0.0328 | 0.0328 | 20 | 0.0172 | 840 | 20 |
| — | 0.0276 | 24 | 0.0141 | 710 | 25 |
| 0.0232 | 0.0232 | 28 | 0.0125 | 590 | 30 |
| — | 0.0195 | 32 | 0.0118 | 500 | 35 |
| 0.0164 | 0.0164 | 35 | 0.0122 | 420 | 40 |
| — | 0.0138 | 42 | 0.0100 | 350 | 45 |
| 0.0116 | 0.0116 | 48 | 0.0092 | 297 | 50 |
| — | 0.0097 | 60 | 0.0070 | 250 | 60 |
| 0.0082 | 0.0082 | 65 | 0.0072 | 210 | 70 |
| — | 0.0069 | 80 | 0.0056 | 177 | 80 |
| 0.0058 | 0.0058 | 100 | 0.0042 | 149 | 100 |
| — | 0.0049 | 115 | 0.0038 | 125 | 120 |
| 0.0041 | 0.0041 | 150 | 0.0026 | 105 | 140 |
| — | 0.0035 | 170 | 0.0024 | 88 | 170 |
| 0.0029 | 0.0029 | 200 | 0.0021 | 74 | 200 |
| — | 0.0024 | 250 | 0.0016 | 62 | 230 |
| 0.0021 | 0.0021 | 270 | 0.0016 | 53 | 270 |
| — | 0.0017 | 325 | 0.0014 | 44 | 325 |
| 0.0015 | 0.0015 | 400 | 0.001 | 37 | 400 |

The Tyler Standard Screen Scale Sieves Series has been expanded to include intermediate sieves for closer sizing which gives a ratio of the forth root of two of 1.189 between openings in successive sieves.

## TABLE 17

| SQUARE, SQUARE ROOTS, AND RECIPROCALS | | | | | | | |
|---|---|---|---|---|---|---|---|
| No. | Square | Square Root | Reciprocal | No. | Square | Square Root | Reciprocal |
| 1 | 1 | 1.00 | 1.000 | 41 | 1681 | 6.40 | .024 |
| 2 | 4 | 1.41 | 0.500 | 42 | 1764 | 6.48 | .024 |
| 3 | 9 | 1.73 | .333 | 43 | 1849 | 6.56 | .023 |
| 4 | 16 | 2.00 | .250 | 44 | 1936 | 6.63 | .023 |
| 5 | 25 | 2.24 | .200 | 45 | 2025 | 6.71 | .022 |
| 6 | 36 | 2.45 | .167 | 46 | 2116 | 6.78 | .022 |
| 7 | 49 | 2.65 | .143 | 47 | 2209 | 6.86 | .021 |
| 8 | 64 | 2.83 | .125 | 48 | 2304 | 6.93 | .021 |
| 9 | 81 | 3.00 | .111 | 49 | 2401 | 7.00 | .020 |
| 10 | 100 | 3.16 | .100 | 50 | 2500 | 7.07 | .020 |
| 11 | 121 | 3.32 | .091 | 51 | 2601 | 7.14 | .020 |
| 12 | 144 | 3.46 | .083 | 52 | 2704 | 7.21 | .019 |
| 13 | 169 | 3.61 | .077 | 53 | 2809 | 7.28 | .019 |
| 14 | 196 | 3.74 | .071 | 54 | 2916 | 7.35 | .019 |
| 15 | 225 | 3.87 | .067 | 55 | 3025 | 7.42 | .018 |
| 16 | 256 | 4.00 | .063 | 56 | 3136 | 7.48 | .018 |
| 17 | 289 | 4.12 | .059 | 57 | 3249 | 7.55 | .018 |
| 18 | 324 | 4.24 | .056 | 58 | 3364 | 7.62 | .017 |
| 19 | 361 | 4.36 | .053 | 59 | 3481 | 7.68 | .017 |
| 20 | 400 | 4.47 | .050 | 60 | 3600 | 7.75 | .017 |
| 21 | 441 | 4.58 | .048 | 61 | 3721 | 7.81 | .016 |
| 22 | 484 | 4.69 | .045 | 62 | 3844 | 7.87 | .016 |
| 23 | 529 | 4.80 | .043 | 63 | 3969 | 7.94 | .016 |
| 24 | 576 | 4.90 | .042 | 64 | 4096 | 8.00 | .016 |
| 25 | 625 | 5.00 | .040 | 65 | 4225 | 8.06 | .015 |
| 26 | 676 | 5.10 | .038 | 66 | 4356 | 8.12 | .015 |
| 27 | 729 | 5.20 | .037 | 67 | 4489 | 8.19 | .015 |
| 28 | 784 | 5.29 | .036 | 68 | 4624 | 8.25 | .015 |
| 29 | 841 | 5.39 | .034 | 69 | 4761 | 8.31 | .014 |
| 30 | 900 | 5.48 | .033 | 70 | 4900 | 8.37 | .014 |
| 31 | 961 | 5.57 | .032 | 71 | 5041 | 8.43 | .014 |
| 32 | 1024 | 5.66 | .031 | 72 | 5184 | 8.49 | .014 |
| 33 | 1089 | 5.74 | .030 | 73 | 5329 | 8.54 | .014 |
| 34 | 1156 | 5.83 | .029 | 74 | 5476 | 8.60 | .014 |
| 35 | 1225 | 5.92 | .029 | 75 | 5625 | 8.66 | .013 |
| 36 | 1296 | 6.00 | .028 | 80 | 6400 | 8.94 | .013 |
| 37 | 1369 | 6.08 | .027 | 85 | 7225 | 9.22 | .012 |
| 38 | 1444 | 6.16 | .026 | 90 | 8100 | 9.49 | .011 |
| 39 | 1521 | 6.24 | .026 | 95 | 9025 | 9.75 | .011 |
| 40 | 1600 | 6.32 | .025 | 100 | 10000 | 10.00 | .010 |

## TABLE 18

| TEMPERATURE CONVERSIONS | |
| --- | --- |
| DEGREE CELSIUS | DEGREE FAHRENHEIT |
| -50 | -58 |
| -40 | -40 |
| -30 | -22 |
| -20 | -4 |
| -10 | 14 |
| -5 | 23 |
| 0 | 32 |
| 5 | 41 |
| 10 | 50 |
| 15 | 59 |
| 20 | 68 |
| 25 | 77 |
| 30 | 86 |
| 35 | 95 |
| 40 | 104 |
| 45 | 113 |
| 50 | 122 |
| 55 | 131 |
| 60 | 140 |
| 65 | 149 |
| 70 | 158 |
| 75 | 167.8 |
| 80 | 176 |
| 85 | 188 |
| 90 | 194 |
| 95 | 203 |
| 100 | 212 |
| 105 | 221 |
| 110 | 230 |
| 115 | 239 |
| 120 | 248 |
| 125 | 257 |
| 150 | 302 |
| 175 | 347 |
| 200 | 392 |

T. degree F = (9/5) X T (degree C) +32
T. degree C = (5/9) X T (degree F) −32

## TABLE 19

| PREFIXES APPLIED TO ALL STANDARD INTERNATIONAL UNITS | | |
|---|---|---|
| Multiples and Submultiples | Prefixes | Symbols |
| $1,000,000,000,000 = 10^{12}$ | tera | T |
| $1,000,000,000 = 10^{9}$ | giga | G |
| $*1,000,000 = 10^{6}$ | mega | M |
| $*1,000 = 10^{3}$ | kilo | k |
| $100 = 10^{2}$ | hecto | h |
| $10 = 10$ | deka | da |
| $0.1 = 10^{-1}$ | deci | d |
| $*0.01 = 10^{-2}$ | centi | c |
| $*0.001 = 10^{-3}$ | milli | m |
| $*0.000\ 001 = 10^{-6}$ | micro | $\mu$ |
| $0.000\ 000\ 001 = 10^{-9}$ | nano | n |
| $0.000\ 000.000.001 = 10^{-12}$ | pico | p |
| $0.000\ 000\ 000\ 000\ 001 = 10^{-15}$ | femto | f |
| $0.000\ 000\ 000\ 000\ 000\ 001 = 10^{-18}$ | atto | a |

*Most commonly used

## TABLE 20

### WEIGHTS AND MEASURES

#### Domestic Weights

|  |  |  |
|---:|:---:|:---|
| 1 grain | = | .002286 ounces = .0001429 pounds |
| 7,000 grains | = | 1 pound |
| 16 ounces | = | 1 pound |
| 2,000 pounds | = | 1 short ton |

#### Metric Weights

|  |  |  |
|---:|:---:|:---|
| 1,000 micrograms (4) | = | 1 milligram (mg) |
| 1,000 milligrams | = | 1 gram (gm) |
| 1,000 grams | = | 1 kilogram (kg) |
| 1,000 kilograms | = | 1 metric ton |

#### Domestic Equivalents of Metric Measures

|  |  |  |
|---:|:---:|:---|
| 1 gram | = | .035274 ounces |
| 1 kilogram | = | 2.204622 pounds |
| 1 metric ton | = | 2,204.622 pounds |
| 1 liter | = | 2.1134 pints, liquid measure |
| 1 liter | = | 1.05671 quarts, liquid measure |
| 1 liter | = | .26418 gallons, liquid measure |

#### Metric Equivalents of Domestic Measure

|  |  |  |
|---:|:---:|:---|
| 1 grain | = | 64.799 milligrams |
| 1 ounce, avoir. | = | 28.3495 grams |
| 1 pound, avoir. | = | 453.5924 grams |
| 1 short ton | = | 907.185 kilograms |
| 1 short ton | = | 0.9072 metric tons |
| 1 pint, liquid measure | = | .47317 liters |
| 1 quart, liquid measure | = | .9463 liters |
| 1 gallon, liquid measure | = | 3.785 liters |

#### Food Weights and Measures

|  |  |  |
|---:|:---:|:---|
| One pinch or dash | = | 1/16 teaspoon |
| 60 drops | = | 1 teaspoon |
| 3 teaspoons | = | 1 tablespoon = ½ oz. liquid |
| 4 tablespoons | = | ¼ cup = 2 oz. liquid |
| 1 gill | = | ½ cup = 4 oz. liquid |
| 1 cup | = | 16 tablespoons = 8 oz. liquid |
| 2 cups | = | 1 pint = 16 oz. liquid |
| 2 pints | = | 1 qt. = 32 oz. liquid |
| 1 liter | = | 1.05 quarts liquid |
| 4 quarts | = | 1 gallon = 128 oz. liquid |
| 31½ gallons | = | 1 barrel |
| 2 barrels | = | 1 hogshead |
| 8 quarts | = | 1 peck |
| 4 pecks | = | 1 bushel |

## REFERENCES

Anon. 1984 Spices of the World Cook Book by McCormick.
McGraw Hill Book Co., NY, NY

Anon. 1989 The ALAMANAC. Edward E. Judge & Son, Inc.
Westminster, MD

Anon. 1989 GLOSSARY-Terms used in Talking about Fats and Oils.    Capital
City Products, Co., Columbus, OH

Anon. 1982 CANNED FOODS, 4th Ed.
Food Processors Institute, Washington, DC

Doyle, Edwin S. and Abe Mittler, 1977. Control of Critical Points in
Food Processing. The Bosley Corporation, Indianapolis, IN

Gould, Wilbur A. and Ronald W. Gould. 1988 Total Quality Assurance
for the Food Industries. CTI Publications, Inc., Baltimore, MD

Gould, Wilbur A. 1990. CGMP's/Food Plant Sanitation. CTI Publications,
Inc., Baltimore, MD

Kramer, A. and B.A., Twigg. 1970. Fundaments of Quality Control for the Food
Industries. 3rd Edition AVI Publishing Co., Inc., Westport, CN

Lopez, A. 1987 A Complete Course in Canning. The Canning Trade Inc.
Baltimore, MD

Mario, Thomas 1978 Quantity Cooking. AVI Publishing Co., Inc.
Westport, CN

Montagne, Prosper 1961 Larousse Gastronomique-The Encyclopeida of
Food, Wine and Cookery. Crown Publishing Inc., NY, NY.

Mountney, George J. and Wilbur A. Gould. 1988 Practical Food
Microbiology and Technology. Van Nostrand Reinhold Company, NY,
NY.

Nelson, Philip E., James V. Chambers, Judy H. Rodriques. 1987 Principles of
Aseptic Processing and Packaging. The Food Processors Institute,
Washington, DC

Ockerman, H.W. 1987 Source Book for Food Scientists. The AVI Publishing
Co. Inc., Westport, CN

Peterson, Martin S. and Arnold H. Johnson. 1978. Encyclopedia of Food
Science. The AVI Publishing Co., Inc. Westport, CN

Wittenberg, M. M. 1987 Experiencing Cooking. Published by Whole Food
Market, Inc., Austin, TX